150 Calorie Desserts

Shame-Free
Recipes to
Satisfy your
Sweet Tooth

Printed in the United States of America
by G&R Publishing Co.

Published By:

Products

507 Industrial Street
Waverly, IA 50677

ISBN-13: 978-1-56383-317-5
ISBN-10: 1-56383-317-4
Item #7105

TABLE OF CONTENTS

THE LOW-DOWN ON LOW-CAL

Are desserts off-limits?

When desserts have a big Mmmm... factor and bring groans of delight to the taster, we often believe they are off-limits for dieters or anyone who is trying to eat sensibly. But the recipes in this book will prove that isn't always true. You don't have to deprive yourself of all yummy sweets – you just need to choose wisely to satisfy both your dieting goals and your sweet tooth.

Everyone knows it's smart to choose foods that are low in calories but high in nutrients. Nutrient-dense foods, like fresh fruits and whole grains, won't add excess calories to your diet, plus they contain vitamins, minerals and fiber to promote good health. Those things help you feel full and satisfied longer than eating the same quantity of "junk" food that is much higher in calories but contains very few nutrients or fiber. And, since junk foods don't stick with you, you tend to be hungry again sooner.

However, sometimes a fresh apple or orange, no matter how juicy and sweet, just won't hit the mark if you're craving something decadent. You may actually be less successful at weight loss or maintenance if you always deprive yourself of tasty desserts. So go ahead, enjoy the recipes in this book, shame-free. They're all 150 calories or less and offer many ways to treat yourself without ruining a healthy, low-calorie eating plan.

What are calories?

A calorie is a unit of measurement, but it doesn't measure length or weight. A calorie is actually a unit of energy. For example, when a portion of food contains 100 calories, that describes how much energy your body gets from eating that portion of food.

If you take in more calories than your body burns, you will gain weight. If you take in fewer calories than you burn, you will lose weight. If you balance the two, you will maintain your weight. The number of calories you need depends primarily on your age, gender and activity level. Consult a doctor or nutritionist to determine what your ideal calorie intake should be.

SMART COMBOS = SENSIBLE INDULGENCES

There are several ways to incorporate desserts into a healthy lifestyle. It's just a question of your preferences – and a little self-control! Use these combinations to create a formula that works for you.

1. Rich Ingredients + Small Portions

If you relish the full flavor of real butter, cream or sugar, go ahead and use small amounts of those ingredients to make desserts. But then cut your servings into small portions. You'll be able to savor the flavor without sending the calorie count soaring skyward.

2. Light Ingredients + Larger Portions

If you prefer a heartier portion of dessert, then choose "light" ingredients such as sugar-free, fat-free or low-fat versions. Use sugar substitutes or low-calorie replacements for calorie-laden ingredients, such as oil. Pages 4 through 11 show you how to do this.

3. Visual Appeal + Presentation = Satisfaction

By making desserts look beautiful, you'll feel more satisfied. It's alright to add that 8-calorie Maraschino cherry on top or a tiny dollop of whipped topping. Just don't overdo it. Or drizzle a teaspoon of chocolate syrup over the dessert and plate, but not 2 tablespoons. Using small portions of carefully chosen garnishes can make each dessert special and satisfying.

Then think about the way you present the dessert. Serve small pieces of dessert in pretty miniature cupcake liners, or cut pieces in wedges or diamonds instead of ordinary squares. Serve desserts on attractive small plates, or invest in 3- to 4-ounce dessert cups and dishes, available from restaurant supply stores. You can treat yourself to decadent-looking desserts without sacrificing your diet goals.

TIPS FOR GUILT-FREE ENJOYMENT

Measure!

Before you can eye it, measure it! To become familiar with what a 1-tablespoon portion of whipped topping looks like, actually measure it out. Take a mind's eye photo of it and file it away for future dessert adventures. By gauging these smaller portions accurately and retraining your brain, you'll be on your way to easy portion control.

Enjoy!

Savor each bite of your dessert. Eat slowly, taking a sip or two of your accompanying beverage between bites. Let the creamy smoothness coat your tongue, or allow the chilled sweetness of a favorite dessert send a shiver down your spine. On those days that you choose to indulge, enjoy it.

Don't feel guilty!

If you're choosing recipes that you love, eating sensible portions, and adding these desserts to an already-balanced diet at reasonable intervals, then it's time to get rid of the guilt. Allow yourself a little indulgence, knowing that it won't blow your diet.

Don't double up!

It may take an extra portion of self-control, but don't take that extra portion of dessert. Even the lowest-calorie desserts can derail your diet goals if you eat three pieces instead of one. Remember to treat sweets like special treats.

Move!

To stay healthy, it's important to exercise. If you want to add more desserts to your diet, it makes sense to add more exercise as well. That can take the form of walking, bicycling, exercise classes, pursuing active hobbies, or just taking opportunities to move rather than sit. Adults should be active for no less than 30 minutes a day for most days of the week. Exercising even more is better.

Super Substitutions

For cooking and baking, there are many lower-calorie foods that can be used as substitutes for high-calorie ingredients. You may prefer to use low-fat, fat-free or sugar-free substitutes in some recipes to reduce calorie counts even more; it's really a personal preference. Here's the scoop on some popular swaps.

Original product	Replace with	Calories Saved
2 T. sweetened whipped cream (55 cal)	2 T. whipped topping, frozen in a carton	
	Regular (25 cal)	30
	Light (20 cal)	35
	Sugar-free, fat-free (15 cal)	40
	2 T. whipped topping in a pressurized can	
	Original (20 cal)	35
	Fat-free (5 cal)	50
1 T. half-and-half cream (20 cal)	1 T. non-dairy creamer, liquid	
	Original (20 cal)	0
	Low-fat or fat-free (10 cal)	10
1 large egg (75 cal)	2 egg whites (32 cal)	43
	¼ cup egg substitute (30 cal)	45
1 T. butter or margarine (100 cal)	1 T. light whipped, 40% fat (75 cal)	25
	1 T. light spread, 37% fat (45 cal)	55
	1 T. fat-free squeeze spread (5 cal)	95

(Note: Whipped and squeeze spreads are not satisfactory for baked products, such as cookies; there is extra water in them. Reduced-fat margarines may be used in some baked products but use only ¾ of the amount of the full-fat margarine listed in the recipe.)

OTHER SUBSTITUTIONS TO TRY

- Substitute 1 cup low-fat buttermilk for 1 cup plain low-fat yogurt to avoid about 45 calories in some sauces or fillings.

- When a recipe calls for heavy cream as a liquid ingredient (not whipped), substitute canned whole evaporated milk for it, tablespoon for tablespoon. This cuts out about 30 calories per tablespoon.

- In baked products, such as cakes, muffins, quick breads and brownies, substitute applesauce, plain low-fat yogurt, pureed prunes* or mashed bananas for half of the shortening, oil or butter in the recipe. Remember that prunes and bananas will add a definite flavor to the product. Homemade or baby food pureed prunes taste good in spice, carrot and chocolate cakes. Bananas work well in banana or carrot cakes or muffins. Applesauce and yogurt taste good in almost any recipe. These substitutions trim off many calories but still produce a moist tender product.

- If you love nuts or coconut but wish to cut calories, toast them first. This brings out their flavor so you can reduce the amount needed, thus cutting out calories.

How-to Tip

To puree prunes yourself, combine 4 ounces of pitted prunes with 3 tablespoons hot water in a blender or food processor. Blend until smooth. This is approximately equal to one (4 ounce) jar of baby food pureed prunes, which can also be used.

SUGAR AND ITS SUBSTITUTES

For people who must limit sugar intake due to diabetes or other health issues, artificial sweeteners can be used in place of sugar or honey in many recipes. Choosing a substitute should be based on personal preferences and how it will be used. Here are things to remember in the sometimes-confusing world of sugar and sugar substitutes.

- The sugar substitutes listed on the next page have been approved by the FDA (Food and Drug Administration).

- All of these sugar substitutes are made by chemical processing so they taste sweet like sugar but have fewer calories. None are naturally-occurring substances.

- Artificial sweeteners are much sweeter than sugar, so it generally takes a smaller amount to give the same sweetness as sugar. Some products, however, have been developed to substitute for sugar in equal amounts. It is important to read the product instructions when deciding which one to buy and how much to use.

- Most sugar substitutes are good for general tabletop use: sprinkling on cereal or stirring into beverages to add sweetness. But not all of them are designed for cooking or baking at high temperatures; some lose their sweetening power. Read the product labels in order to choose substitutes that fit your needs.

- In most desserts that are not baked, you can reduce the amount of real sugar by 25% and add a pinch of ground spice, such as cinnamon or allspice for added flavor and fewer calories.

- Real sugar does more than sweeten. In baked products, it contributes moisture, texture, browning and volume. Generally, you may replace half of the sugar in a favorite recipe with a sugar substitute and still achieve a good-quality baked product.

- Some manufacturers are developing special recipes and offering special tips to successfully make baked goods using their products to replace all sugar. Check their websites for more information.

- As with natural sugar, it's best to consume processed sugar substitutes in moderation.

Chemical Name	Brand Names	Forms	Uses		
			General	Baking	Cooking
Aspartame	Equal Equal Spoonful NutraSweet NatraTaste	• powdered (blue packets) • granulated	X	not recommended for high temperatures or long cooking times*	
Acesulfame-K (also called Acesulfame-potassium or Ace-K)	Sweet One	• powdered (blue, yellow, & red packets)	X	X**	X**
Saccharin	Sweet 'N Low Brown Sweet 'N Low Sugar Twin	• powdered (pink packets) • granulated • liquid	X	X**	X**
Sucralose	Splenda	• powdered (yellow packets) • granulated	X	X	X

* This product is best when added at the end of the cooking time, or it can be used in specially-created baking recipes. It may have less sweetness when heated to high temperatures in standard recipes.

** Some people notice an aftertaste when using this artificial sweetener in cooked or baked products.

> *Since the caloric value in sugar substitutes is very small per serving, the FDA considers it "insignificant" and these products can call themselves "no calorie" or "zero calorie" sweeteners even though they contain trace calories.*

New sweeteners are being developed all the time. For example, neotame has been approved for use in foods like chewing gum, soft drinks and candy, and companies are testing natural sweeteners made from the South American stevia plant. There are also blends that combine sugar with artificial sweeteners in one product.

Mock Whipped Topping

Makes about 4 cups

1 tsp. unflavored gelatin powder

½ C. skim milk

½ C. instant nonfat dry milk powder

1 T. sugar

½ tsp. vanilla extract

Chill a small mixing bowl and electric beaters. In another small bowl, soften gelatin in 2 teaspoons water for 5 minutes. Meanwhile, in a small saucepan over medium-low heat, combine skim milk and nonfat dry milk powder; stir and heat until simmering. Add softened gelatin and stir until dissolved. Remove from heat and stir in sugar and vanilla until well blended. Chill until mixture begins to thicken. Transfer mixture to chilled mixing bowl and beat at high speed with the electric mixer until very thick and light, about 5 minutes. Best if used immediately, but may be stored in an airtight container for several days.

Serving size: *2 tablespoons*
Calories: *11*
Fat: *trace fat*

Low-Cal Whipped Topping

Makes about 6 cups

1 (20 oz.) can evaporated skim milk, chilled
1 T. honey
1½ tsp. vanilla extract

Chill a large mixing bowl and electric beaters. Pour milk into bowl and use the electric mixer at high speed to beat until foamy. Add honey and vanilla; continue to beat until mixture is the consistency of whipped cream. Use immediately.

Serving size: *2 tablespoons*
Calories: *12*
Fat: *0 g*

Yogurt-Ricotta Whipped Topping

Makes about 1 cup

3 T. plain low-fat yogurt
¾ C. part-skim ricotta cheese
1 tsp. vanilla extract
2 packets sugar substitute

In a small deep bowl, use an electric mixer at medium speed to beat together yogurt and ricotta cheese until smooth and creamy. Add vanilla and sugar substitute; beat until mixture is thoroughly blended. Refrigerate until ready to serve. Whip again before serving.

Serving size: *2 tablespoons*
Calories: *35*
Fat: *1.3 g*

Sweetened Condensed Milk Substitute

Makes about ¾ cup

1⅓ C. instant nonfat dry milk powder
½ C. Splenda sugar substitute

In a microwave-safe bowl, combine non-fat dry milk powder with ½ cup water to make a paste. Cover and cook on high power for 45 seconds or until hot but not boiling. Remove from microwave and stir in sugar substitute. Cover and chill in refrigerator for at least 2 hours before using. Store in an airtight container for up to 2 weeks.

Serving size: *1 tablespoon*
Calories: *14*
Fat: *0 g*

Dieter's Sour Cream

Makes about 1¼ cups

2 T. skim milk
1 T. lemon juice
1 C. low-fat cottage cheese

In a blender container, combine milk, lemon juice and cottage cheese. Blend at medium-high speed until smooth and creamy. Chill well before using.

Serving size: *1 tablespoon*
Calories: *9*
Fat: *trace fat*

Tip: For use in hot dishes, add just before serving.

Creamy Pudding & Pie Filling

Makes about 2¼ cups

1½ tsp. unflavored gelatin powder
1½ C. skim milk, divided
1½ T. cornstarch
3 egg yolks
¼ C. honey
1½ tsp. vanilla extract

Place ¾ cup cold water in a small saucepan. Sprinkle gelatin over water and set aside to soften for 5 minutes. Heat 1¼ cups milk in a medium saucepan over medium-low heat until hot. In a jar with a tight-fitting lid, combine remaining ¼ cup milk and cornstarch and shake together until well blended; set aside. In a small bowl, beat egg yolks with honey until well mixed and lemon-colored. Beat in cornstarch mixture. Stir a small amount of the hot milk into egg yolk mixture. Gradually stir in more milk until egg mixture is warmed. Transfer back to pan with remaining milk mixture and heat, whisking constantly, until pudding coats the back of a wooden spoon. Remove from heat. Heat softened gelatin in saucepan until it dissolves. Stir gelatin mixture into creamy mixture. Add vanilla and mix well. Cool slightly before placing into dessert dishes or prepared pie crust of choice.

Serving size: *about ¼ cup*
Calories: *74*
Fat: *1.7 g*

Variations
• *Pour slightly-cooled filling into a low-calorie graham cracker crust, chill and serve. Top pie or pudding cups with ½ cup toasted coconut (directions on page 28), sliced bananas or another fruit. Try drizzling chocolate or strawberry syrup on top.*

Questions & Answers

Q: Why do some desserts in this book use real sugar, honey and butter rather than low-calorie substitutes?

A: Some recipes contain regular sweeteners and fat, causing the overall calorie count to be higher than they would be with low-calorie substitutes. These desserts will be satisfying and may stick with you longer. But the secret to correctly adding them to your diet is portion size. Eaten in small portions, these recipes allow your taste buds to savor full flavor, yet restrict the calories so you won't blow your total calorie count in one sitting. Other dessert recipes make use of the wide variety of tasty sugar substitutes and low-fat or fat-free products available today. This allows larger portions but the satiety value may be reduced. You may choose to make substitutions according to your preferences.

Q: Is it healthier to use real sweetened whipping cream, whipped toppings in frozen tubs, or refrigerated toppings in aerosol cans?

A: In limited quantities, all of those products are alright. Although the whipped toppings are usually made from partially hydrogenated oil, sweeteners, plus other man-made ingredients, most contain less total fat than homemade sweetened whipped cream. If you are just trying to cut out fat, a fat-free version of whipped topping might be the best choice. If you prefer natural ingredients, choose whipping cream.

Q: When a label says "light", what does that mean?

A: The calorie count should be lower than the "original" food and/or it will contain less fat. It may also contain less sodium. Technically, the labels can also be used to mean "light in color" or "light in texture" but that would need to be explained on the label. Sometimes "light" or "lite" foods actually contain more sugar, so be sure to read all food labels well.

Q: What does "fat-free" really mean?

A: For a product to wear the label of "fat-free", it must contain less than 0.5 grams of total fat in one serving.

Q: Can I ever order desserts in restaurants?

A: Many restaurants offer lower-calorie or miniature versions of rich desserts. See page 16 for a list of low-calorie choices, or ask if the restaurant can provide nutritional information.

QUICK-PICK LISTS

What's a quick way to judge a dessert? Consider the "4 C's" each time you're tempted to indulge your sweet tooth. Try to avoid desserts described as Creamy, Crunchy, Crispy or Chewy. Although these four words don't automatically equate to high calories, they sure are a good indication that the items might not be your best choice. They hint at high fat and sugar content unless low-calorie substitution ingredients are used.

And, as with all desserts, size matters. Choose a small portion, like Snack- or Fun-size servings rather than Jumbo, Giant, Extra-Large, Super-size, King-size or Big. Then your little indulgence won't ruin your dedication to a low-calorie diet.

Best Choices for Ice Cream Lovers

Choose this...	...not this.
vanilla soft serve	large white chocolate mousse
child-sized serving	large serving
sorbet or sherbet	extra-creamy, extra-rich ice cream
fresh fruit toppings or mix-ins	candy, cookie dough or nut toppings or mix-ins
cake cone	sugar or waffle cone
1 fudge bar	1 Dilly Bar
1 no-sugar-added vanilla ice cream sandwich	1 chocolate chip cookie ice cream sandwich
1 Dove Ice Cream Miniature	1 Dove Ice Cream Bar
1 small scoop chocolate ice cream	1 small scoop peanut butter cup ice cream
strawberry or other fruit toppings	hot fudge or caramel toppings

Quick-Pick Lists

Best Choices for Candy Lovers

Choose this…	…not this.
1 fun-size chocolate candy bar	1 giant chocolate Chunky Bar
1 wrapped caramel	1 caramel-filled chocolate bar
3 Rolo caramel-filled chocolates	1 king-size Twix bar
1 milk chocolate kiss	1 full-size milk chocolate bar
10 Lemonheads	3 chocolate truffles
1 fun-size bag Skittles	1 king-size bag Skittles
1 roll Smarties	3 candy orange slices
3 butterscotch disks	1 bag Sugar Babies
2 licorice Twizzlers	5 pieces salt-water taffy
8 Junior Mints	1 (1.37 oz.) York peppermint patty

Best Choices for Cake and Pie Lovers

Choose this…	…not this.
pie with 1 crust	pie with 2 crusts
fruit pie	creamy pie with multiple layers
whipped frostings	rich and creamy supreme frostings
1 piece angel food cake	1 piece pound cake
1 low-fat brownie	1 cheesecake swirl brownie
1 Little Debbie Swiss Cake Roll	1 Little Debbie Boston Crème Roll
1 small cupcake	1 piece iced carrot cake
1 piece lemon cake	1 wedge cheesecake with fruit
1 piece lower-fat cake, glazed	1 piece "poke" cake with sweetened condensed milk or ice cream fillings, frosted
1 Hostess Ho-Ho	1 Hostess Brownie
1 slice pumpkin pie	1 slice French silk or pecan pie

Quick-Pick Lists

Best Choices for Cookie Monsters

Choose this…	…not this.
1 Chips Ahoy! regular chocolate chip cookie (crisp)	1 chewy or chunky chocolate chip version
1 reduced-fat Oreo cookie	1 Double-Stuf Oreo cookie
1 iced oatmeal cookie	1 Archway Home Style oatmeal cookie
5 vanilla wafers	2 vanilla cream-filled sandwich cookies
5 iced animal crackers	5 shortbread or butter cookies
1 chocolate biscotti	1 Little Debbie Nutty Bar
2 gingersnap cookies	1 peanut butter cookie
1 fudge-striped cookie	1 double-fudge cookie
1 lemon cookie	1 monster M&M cookie
1 Pepperidge Farm Lido cookie	1 Pepperidge Farm Chocolate-Dipped Nantucket

Other Tips

• Baking Tip: Reduce the calories in made-from-scratch cookies or cookies baked from refrigerated dough simply by making each cookie smaller.

• Cookie cravings? Low calorie choices for your sweet tooth include ginger snaps, graham crackers, vanilla wafers, unfrosted animal crackers and fig-filled cookies. Avoid cookies filled with chocolate chips, peanut butter and other sweet, gooey stuff.

RESTAURANT DESSERT PICKS: HIGHS AND LOWS

You can indulge in dessert at restaurants if you choose wisely and avoid the calorie-laden ones. Here is a sampling of low-calorie choices and their extremely high counterpoints.

Restaurant	Choose this…	…not this.
TCBY	One small serving of non-fat frozen yogurt (110 calories)	Lotta Colada Smoothie with yogurt (550 calories)
Baskin Robbins	One regular scoop flavored ice or sorbet (115 to 135 calories). Add a cake cone (25 additional calories)	York Peppermint Pattie Brownie Sundae (1,610 calories)
Au Bon Pain	One large fruit cup (12 oz.) (140 calories)	One blonde brownie with nuts (570 calories)
Pizza Hut	One cinnamon stick with white icing dip (160 calories)	One slice apple dessert pizza (260 calories)
Dunkin Donuts	One French cruller (150 calories)	One peanut butter cup cookie (590 calories)
Jamba Juice	Strawberry Nirvana Light Smoothie (250 calories)	Peanut Butter Moo'd Smoothie (840 calories)
Denny's	One scoop of ice cream with cherry topping (245 calories)	One piece of carrot cake (800 calories)
Chili's	Sweet Shots, Strawberry Wave Cheesecake (220 calories)	Chocolate Chip Paradise Pie with Vanilla Ice Cream (1,600 calories)

Other Tips

• On a dessert menu, certain words are usually synonymous with higher calories. Try to avoid desserts with these description words: "chocolate", "brownie", "cookie", "fudge", "candy pieces", "caramel", "nutty", "truffle", or "double-fudge".

• If you're in the mood for pie, choose a fruit pie with one crust. You'll get nutrients and fiber from the fruit and consume fewer fat calories with only a single crust.

Simply Fruity

Fruit Kabobs with Creamy Dip

Makes 8 servings

¾ C. honeydew melon chunks

¾ C. cantaloupe chunks

¾ C. small strawberries, hulled

¾ C. fresh pineapple chunks

2 small bananas, peeled and cut into 1" slices

1 C. orange juice

¼ C. lime juice

1 C. low-fat or fat-free vanilla yogurt

2 T. frozen orange juice concentrate, thawed

¼ tsp. ground nutmeg or cinnamon, optional

On eight 6" skewers, alternately thread the honeydew melon, cantaloupe, strawberries, pineapple and bananas. Place kabobs in a glass baking dish; set aside. In a small bowl, combine orange juice and lime juice; pour evenly over fruit kabobs. Cover and chill in refrigerator for 30 to 60 minutes, turning occasionally. Meanwhile, prepare the dip by combining yogurt and orange juice concentrate in a small serving bowl. Stir well, cover and chill until ready to serve. Remove fruit kabobs from baking dish and arrange on a serving platter; discard juice marinade. Set bowl of dip on platter and sprinkle nutmeg or cinnamon over dip, if desired.

Serving size: 1 kabob and about 2 tablespoons dip
Calories: 91
Fat: 1 g

Honeyed Fruit Kabobs

12 fresh pineapple chunks
12 strawberries, hulled
12 large green grapes
2 medium bananas, each cut into 6 bite-size pieces
½ C. orange juice
⅓ C. honey
1 T. lemon juice
⅛ tsp. mint extract

On a 6" skewer, thread a pineapple chunk, strawberry, grape and banana piece to make one fruit kabob. Repeat to make 11 more kabobs. Place all skewers into a 9x13" baking dish. In a small bowl, combine orange juice, honey, lemon juice and mint extract; stir well. Pour mixture over fruit kabobs. Cover and refrigerate for 2 hours, turning occasionally. Remove kabobs from dish and serve immediately. Discard marinade.

Serving size: *1 kabob*
Calories: *80*
Fat: *0 g*

Blueberry-Stuffed Apples

Makes 4 servings

4 medium apples
2 T. maple syrup
½ C. fresh blueberries
¼ C. fat-free whipped topping

Preheat oven to 350°. Wash and core apples, but replace a 1″ plug from removed core back into the bottom of each apple. Do not peel. Place apples, open end up, in a shallow baking dish. In a small bowl, combine maple syrup and blueberries until berries are well-coated. Stuff apples with blueberry mixture and bake for about 30 minutes or until apples are soft. Top each stuffed apple with 1 tablespoon of whipped topping and serve warm.

Serving size: *1 apple*
Calories: *111*
Fat: *0 g*

How-to Tip

- *The best apples to choose for the tastiest desserts will be labeled U.S. Extra Fancy, Fancy or No. 1.*
- *U.S. Low-grade apples are labeled U.S. No. 2.*

Spiced Fruit Dip

Makes 8 servings

2 tsp. Sweet 'N Low brown sugar substitute
½ tsp. ground cinnamon
½ tsp. ground allspice
¼ tsp. ground nutmeg
1 C. heavy whipping cream
Fresh fruit, cut into bite-size pieces

In a small bowl, combine brown sugar substitute, cinnamon, allspice and nutmeg; mix well and set aside. In a chilled mixing bowl using chilled beaters, beat cream until almost stiff. Gently fold in spice mixture and transfer to a serving bowl. Refrigerate until ready to serve. Spear fresh fruit pieces with toothpicks and serve them with the dip.

Serving size: *2 tablespoons dip*
Calories: *106*
Fat: *11 g*

Shame-Free

To cut calories and fat, replace the heavy whipping cream with Yogurt-Ricotta Whipped Topping (recipe on page 9), but omit sugar substitute. You may also stir the spices into a small tub of low-fat or fat-free whipped topping and cut brown sugar substitute in half.

Velvety Chocolate Dip

Makes 6 servings

6 T. fat-free plain yogurt
6 T. fat-free chocolate syrup
1 tsp. frozen orange juice concentrate, thawed
Fresh strawberries or other fruit

In a small mixing bowl, whisk together yogurt, chocolate syrup and orange juice concentrate. Cover and chill. Serve with fresh strawberries.

Serving size: *2 tablespoons dip*
Calories: *63*
Fat: *0 g*

Shame-Free

The wise use of extracts and flavorings can make low-calorie desserts taste richer and more satisfying. Since they don't have many calories, you can use them generously to bring out the flavor of other foods. Store them in a cool, dark place, tightly closed, to maintain flavor.

Balsamic Strawberries over Ice Cream

1 T. light butter (40% fat)
2 C. fresh strawberries, hulled and halved
¼ C. granulated Splenda
1 T. balsamic vinegar
4 (½ C.) scoops fat-free vanilla ice cream

In a large skillet over medium heat, melt butter. Add strawberries, Splenda and balsamic vinegar. Cook until strawberries are heated through and darkened to a ruby red, stirring gently. To serve, place ½ cup of ice cream into each of four dessert bowls or stemmed glasses. Spoon strawberries and sauce over ice cream.

Serving size: *1 small dessert bowl*
Calories: *149*
Fat: *2.1 g*

Variation

• *Serve Balsamic Strawberries over frozen yogurt, angel food cake or inside crepes.*

Refreshing Summer Fruit Blend

Makes 12 servings

2 (0.3 oz.) pkgs. sugar-free strawberry gelatin powder

1½ C. diet ginger ale, cold

1 C. sliced fresh strawberries

1 C. green grapes, halved

1 C. cantaloupe chunks

In a microwave-safe bowl, bring 2 cups of water to a boil. Place gelatin powder into a large bowl; add boiling water and stir 2 minutes or until gelatin is completely dissolved. Stir in cold ginger ale until blended. Refrigerate about 1½ hours or until thickened but not completely set. Stir in strawberries, grapes and cantaloupe. Pour mixture into a 2-quart serving bowl and refrigerate 4 hours or until firm.

Serving size: *about ½ cup*
Calories: *25*
Fat: *0 g*

Variations

- *Use cherry gelatin or another red sugar-free gelatin in place of strawberry.*
- *Substitute cold water or diet red raspberry soda for the ginger ale.*
- *Top with a dollop of whipped topping before serving.*

Creamy Strawberry-Orange Cups

Makes 6 servings

2 C. fresh strawberries, hulled and halved
1 env. unflavored gelatin powder
½ C. frozen orange juice concentrate, thawed
1½ C. skim milk
1 tsp. vanilla extract
1 T. sugar, optional

Cut half of the strawberries into thin slices. Place a few slices into the bottoms of six 8-ounce custard or dessert cups, dividing them equally. In a small bowl, combine 2 tablespoons cool water and gelatin; let stand 5 minutes to soften. Add 2 tablespoons boiling water to softened gelatin and stir until completely dissolved. In a separate bowl, combine orange juice concentrate, milk, vanilla and sugar; mix well. Add the dissolved gelatin to milk mixture and stir well. Pour mixture evenly over sliced strawberries in custard cups. Refrigerate cups for 2 hours or until completely set. Use remaining strawberry halves to garnish top of each dessert cup.

Serving size: *1 dessert cup*
Calories: *90*
Fat: *0.3 g*

Variation

• *Use raspberries in place of strawberries.*

Cran-Raspberry Gelatin

2 (0.3 oz.) pkgs. sugar-free raspberry gelatin powder

1¾ C. light cranberry-raspberry juice, divided

1¼ C. whole-berry cranberry sauce

1 (20 oz.) can crushed pineapple packed in juice, undrained

2½ C. frozen unsweetened raspberries, thawed

1 C. reduced-fat sour cream

2 T. brown sugar

1 C. reduced-fat whipped topping

Coat a 7 x 11" baking dish with cooking spray; set aside. Empty both packages of gelatin into a large bowl. Bring 1 cup of cranberry-raspberry juice to a boil and pour hot juice over gelatin, stirring until completely dissolved. Add cranberry sauce and stir to break up sauce and blend mixture well. Stir in remaining ¾ cup cranberry-raspberry juice, mixing thoroughly. Cover and refrigerate for 1½ hours or until partially set. Remove from refrigerator and fold in pineapple with juice and raspberries. Transfer mixture to prepared dish and refrigerate until firm. Before serving, combine sour cream and brown sugar in a small bowl, mixing well. Fold in whipped topping. Spread mixture over gelatin, cut into eight pieces and serve immediately.

Serving size: *1 piece*
Calories: *148*
Fat: *2 g*

Cran-Peach Blueberry Mold

2 env. unflavored gelatin powder
Sugar substitute equal to ¼ C. sugar
2 C. light cranberry juice, chilled
2 fresh peaches, peeled, pitted and cut into chunks
1½ C. fresh blueberries

Coat a 7-cup mold or 2-quart bowl with nonstick cooking spray; set aside. Place 1½ cups cold water in a small saucepan. Sprinkle both envelopes of gelatin over water; let stand for 1 minute. Add sugar substitute. Cook and stir over medium heat until mixture is warm and ingredients dissolve. Do not boil. Transfer to a medium bowl and stir in cranberry juice. Cover and refrigerate until slightly thickened. Remove from refrigerator and fold in peaches and blueberries. Transfer mixture to prepared mold or bowl. Refrigerate until firm. Unmold onto a plate or serving platter.

Serving size: *about 1 cup*
Calories: *70*
Fat: *0 g*

How-to Tip

Peel and cut peaches just before combining with gelatin to avoid browning.

Pineapple Ambrosia

Makes 8 servings

2 C. fresh pineapple chunks

2 oranges, peeled and cut into segments

1 C. sliced strawberries

½ C. sweetened flaked coconut, toasted *

¼ C. chopped macadamia nuts

2 (6 oz.) cartons fat-free piña colada yogurt

In a medium bowl, combine pineapple chunks, orange segments and sliced strawberries. In a separate bowl, mix toasted coconut and nuts. In eight small parfait glasses, alternate layers of fruit, yogurt and coconut mixture.

* To toast, place coconut in a single layer on a shallow baking sheet. Bake at 350° for approximately 7 to 10 minutes, stirring frequently, until coconut is golden brown.

Serving size: *1 parfait*
Calories: *141*
Fat: *5.4 g*

Melon-Sorbet Parfaits

Makes 4 servings

¾ C. seeded watermelon balls

¾ C. seeded cantaloupe melon balls

¾ C. seeded honeydew melon balls

1 C. lemon sorbet

½ C. sweet sparkling wine, fruit-flavored sparkling
water or ginger ale, chilled

Mint sprigs, optional

Chill melon balls for at least 1 hour. Divide melon balls among four stemmed parfait glasses or wine goblets. Scoop ¼ cup sorbet on top of melon balls in each glass. Pour 2 tablespoons of sparkling wine, water or ginger ale over sorbet and melon. Garnish with mint sprigs, if desired. Serve immediately.

Serving size: *1 parfait*
Calories: *91*
Fat: *0 g*

Mango & Cream Parfaits

Makes 4 servings

¼ C. soy milk
1 nectarine, peeled, pitted and chopped
2 T. powdered sugar
½ C. fat-free sour cream
2 ripe mangoes
1 sliced kiwifruit or 4 fresh raspberries

In a blender, combine soy milk, nectarine and powdered sugar. Cover and blend until mixture is smooth. Pour into a medium bowl; stir in sour cream. Cover and chill for 1 hour. Pit and peel mangoes. Cut fruit into ½" cubes. Alternately layer mango pieces and sour cream mixture in four parfait glasses or wine goblets until each glass is full. Top each serving with a spoonful of sour cream mixture. Garnish each serving with a slice of kiwifruit or a fresh raspberry.

Serving size: *1 parfait*
Calories: *128*
Fat: *1.7 g*

Warm-Weather Fruit Cups

½ C. sugar
1 tsp. finely shredded lemon peel
¼ C. loosely packed fresh mint leaves, divided
2 C. sliced fresh apricots
2 C. sliced fresh nectarines
1 C. fresh blackberries

In a medium saucepan over medium heat, combine 1 cup water with sugar, lemon peel and half of the mint leaves. Cook and stir until mixture is bubbly; reduce heat. Cover pan and simmer for 10 minutes. Strain, discarding lemon peel and mint leaves; cool completely. To serve, combine fruit and remaining mint leaves in a large bowl. Drizzle the cooled syrup over the fruit mixture; toss well. Serve immediately or cover and chill in the refrigerator for up to 3 hours.

Serving size: *about ½ cup*
Calories: *96*
Fat: *0 g*

Variations

• *Use sugar substitute in place of sugar to reduce calories further.*
• *Substitute fresh raspberries or boysenberries for the blackberries.*

Refreshing Papaya Fluff

1 very ripe papaya
⅓ C. evaporated skim milk, chilled
1 T. honey
½ tsp. orange extract
2 thin orange slices, cut in half, optional

Peel and seed papaya. Cut fruit into small chunks, reserving 4 small pieces. Place papaya chunks into a blender or food processor and puree until almost smooth. In a medium mixing bowl, use an electric mixer to whip evaporated milk until foamy. Add honey and orange extract; beat until stiff peaks form. Beat in papaya puree until well blended. Spoon into four chilled stemmed dessert dishes, mounding slightly; garnish with a reserved papaya piece and/or half orange slice on top.

Serving size: *1 dessert dish*
Calories: *64*
Fat: *0 g*

Peach Tart

1 C. flour
¼ tsp. salt
¼ C. margarine
1 (8 oz.) pkg. fat-free cream cheese, softened
Sugar substitute equal to ¼ C. sugar
1 tsp. vanilla extract
4 or 5 peaches, peeled, pitted and sliced
½ C. blueberries
½ C. low-calorie apricot spread

Preheat oven to 450°. For pastry, combine flour and salt in a medium bowl. Use a pastry blender or two knives to cut in margarine until crumbly and pieces are the size of small peas. Sprinkle 1 tablespoon cold water over mixture and toss with a fork; repeat with 3 to 4 additional tablespoons of cold water just until mixture is moistened and can be formed into a ball. Place flattened pastry ball on a lightly floured surface; roll out with a floured rolling pin to make a 12" circle. Ease pastry circle into a 10" tart pan with removable bottom; avoid stretching pastry. Press pastry about ½" up sides of pan. Prick bottom well with fork tines. Bake for 12 to 15 minutes or until golden. Cool completely on a wire rack. Remove sides of tart pan. Meanwhile, in a medium mixing bowl combine cream cheese, sugar substitute and vanilla. Beat at medium speed until smooth; spread mixture over cooled pastry. Arrange the sliced peaches over cream cheese layer. Sprinkle blueberries on top of peaches. In a small saucepan over low heat, warm apricot spread until melted, cutting up any large pieces of fruit. Spoon melted spread over blueberries. Chill for 2 to 3 hours. To serve, cut into 12 small wedges.

Serving size: *1 wedge*
Calories: *125*
Fat: *4 g*

Grilled Peachy-Pineapple Crisp

Makes 8 servings

4 C. peeled, thinly sliced peaches

1 (8 oz.) can pineapple tidbits, packed in juice, undrained

¼ C. plus 2 T. brown sugar, divided

1 tsp. quick-cooking tapioca

½ C. quick-cooking oats

¼ C. flour

½ tsp. ground cinnamon

⅛ tsp. ground nutmeg

2 T. light butter, chilled

½ C. fat-free whipped topping, optional

In a medium bowl, combine peaches, pineapple, 2 tablespoons brown sugar and tapioca; stir to mix well. Spoon mixture into an 8" square metal or foil baking pan; set aside. In a separate small bowl, combine remaining ¼ cup brown sugar, flour, cinnamon and nutmeg; stir well. Cut in butter until mixture resembles coarse crumbs. Sprinkle mixture over fruit in pan. Cover pan tightly with foil; place on grill over medium heat until mixture is hot and bubbly, about 50 minutes. Top each serving of warm dessert with 1 tablespoon of fat-free whipped topping.

Serving size: *about ½ cup*
Calories: *149*
Fat: *3 g*

Variations

- *To reduce calories further, use brown sugar substitute and whole wheat flour.*
- *If desired, serve with a small scoop of frozen fat-free vanilla yogurt or ice cream in place of whipped topping, though this will add calories.*

Black Cherry Baked Apples

Makes 4 servings

4 baking apples
½ tsp. ground cinnamon
¼ C. dried cherries
¼ C. chopped walnuts
1 C. diet black cherry soda

Preheat oven to 375°. Wash and core apples, but replace a 1" plug from removed core back into the bottom of each apple. Do not peel. Place apples, open end up, in a 9" square baking dish. Sprinkle inside of apples with cinnamon. Spoon an equal portion of cherries and walnuts into each apple. Drizzle a little soda into each apple and pour the remaining soda into the baking dish. Bake for 20 minutes or until apples are tender.

Serving size: *1 apple*
Calories: *146*
Fat: *4.6 g*

How-to Tip

Apples can be stored in the refrigerator for several weeks, but keep them away from fresh vegetables. Apples give off ethylene gas and that can cause vegetables to spoil.

Poached Pears
with Raspberry Sauce

Makes 8 servings

4 firm Bosc pears, peeled

½ C. seedless low-calorie raspberry fruit spread

1 C. apple juice

2 tsp. finely shredded lemon peel

2 T. lemon juice

2 C. nonfat frozen vanilla yogurt

Cut pears into fourths. In a 10" nonstick skillet, mix raspberry spread, apple juice, lemon peel and lemon juice; stir well. Add pears and heat mixture to boiling. Reduce heat to medium and simmer uncovered for 20 to 30 minutes, turning and basting pears with juice occasionally. Place a small scoop of frozen yogurt (about ¼ cup) into 8 dessert dishes. Spoon warm pears over yogurt and serve immediately.

Serving size: *2 pear pieces with ¼ cup frozen yogurt*
Calories: *144*
Fat: *0 g*

Frozen
Favorites

Fresh Orange Sorbet

2 C. freshly squeezed orange juice
3 T. honey
1¼ tsp. orange extract

Strain orange juice into a large bowl to remove pulp. Add 1½ cups water and set aside. In a small saucepan, heat ½ cup water and honey until honey dissolves. Add mixture to the large bowl with juice and stir in orange extract, mixing well. Place mixture into the container of an ice cream maker and process according to manufacturer's instructions.

Alternate method: Pour mixture into a large pan or bowl and place in freezer until mushy. Remove from freezer, beat with a large spoon to break down ice crystals and return pan to freezer. Repeat this procedure twice, then freeze until ready to serve.

Serving size: ½ cup
Calories: 53
Fat: 0 g

Watermelon and Berry Sorbet

Makes 6 servings

½ C. sugar

2 C. seedless watermelon cubes

2 C. fresh strawberries, hulled and halved

1 T. minced fresh mint

In a small heavy saucepan, combine sugar with 1 cup water. Bring mixture to a boil and cook until sugar dissolves, stirring often. Remove from heat and cool slightly. Place watermelon and strawberries in a blender; add sugar syrup. Cover and process for 2 to 3 minutes or until smooth. Strain and discard seeds and pulp. Transfer puree to a 9 x 13" baking dish. Freeze for 1 hour or until edges begin to get firm. Remove from freezer and stir in mint. Freeze for 2 more hours or until firm. Just before serving, transfer mixture to a blender. Cover and process for 2 to 3 minutes or until smooth. Serve in dessert dishes.

Serving size: *½ cup*
Calories: *95*
Fat: *0 g*

Mixed-Fruit Sorbet Cones

Makes 7 servings

2 C. frozen blueberries
2 C. frozen raspberries
¼ C. frozen pineapple-orange-banana juice concentrate
7 sugar cones

In a large bowl, combine both berries, frozen juice concentrate and ½ cup water. Place half of mixture into a food processor. Cover and process until almost smooth. Transfer blended mixture to a baking dish. Process remaining fruit mixture and add to same dish; stir blended portions together. Cover and freeze for 4 hours or until firm. Scoop mixture into cones and serve immediately.

Serving size: *½ cup*
Calories: *116*
Fat: *0 g*

Papaya Sorbet

Makes 4 servings

1 ripe papaya, diced (about 1¼ lbs.)
¼ C. plain low-fat yogurt
½ C. light corn syrup
1 tsp. fresh lime juice

Arrange papaya in a 9" square baking pan; freeze for 1 hour. Place frozen papaya in a food processor with yogurt, corn syrup and lime juice. Process until smooth. Place mixture back into baking pan and freeze for at least 1 hour. Scoop into small dessert cups.

Serving size: *½ cup*
Calories: *97*
Fat: *0.8 g*

Lovely Lemon Ice

Makes 4 servings

1 (0.3 oz.) pkg. sugar-free lemon gelatin powder
1 C. diet lemon-lime seltzer
½ tsp. grated lemon peel
3 T. fresh lemon juice
Lemon slices
Mint leaves, optional

Place lemon gelatin in a medium bowl. Add 1 cup boiling water and stir for 2 minutes or until gelatin is completely dissolved. Add seltzer, lemon peel and lemon juice; stir well. Pour mixture into a 9″ square pan. Cover pan and freeze for 3 hours or until firm. Remove pan from freezer and let stand at room temperature for 10 minutes to soften slightly. Spoon into a mixing bowl and beat with an electric mixer, or put into a blender and blend on high speed until smooth. Spoon into four dessert dishes and garnish with lemon slices and mint leaves, if desired.

Serving size: *about ½ cup*
Calories: *13*
Fat: *0 g*

Variations

- *Spoon mixture into ice cube trays, freeze completely and store cubes in baggies. To serve, blend six to eight cubes for 2 servings.*
- *Make Peach Ice by using sugar-free peach gelatin in place of lemon and diet peach-flavored seltzer in place of lemon-lime seltzer.*
- *Make Black Cherry Ice by using sugar-free black cherry gelatin in place of lemon and diet black cherry seltzer in place of lemon-lime seltzer.*

Peach Almond Ice

Makes 8 servings

3 C. peeled, sliced fresh peaches
½ C. honey
1½ tsp. almond extract

In a large saucepan, bring 2 cups of water to a boil. Add peaches, reduce heat and cook peaches until soft, about 10 minutes. Drain peaches, reserving juice; set aside to cool. In a food processor, puree cooled peaches. Add reserved juice, honey and almond extract; process until blended. Pour peach mixture into the container of an ice cream maker and process according to manufacturer's instructions. Alternately, place mixture into a large shallow bowl and place into freezer until thickened but not frozen. Remove from freezer and beat mixture with a large spoon to break down ice crystals, then return to freezer. Repeat this process two times, spooning mixture into an airtight storage container the last time. Freeze until ready to serve.

Serving size: *about ½ cup*
Calories: *84*
Fat: *0 g*

Sunset Granita

Makes 5 servings

3 oranges

1 small tub low-calorie orange-flavored soft drink mix powder (like Crystal Light)

1 (12 oz.) bag frozen raspberries

Cut the oranges in half. Scoop out the pulp from each orange half, leaving the shells intact. Set the shells aside and use the removed pulp for another recipe. In a large pitcher, dissolve drink mix in 1¼ cups water, mixing well. Pour half of beverage into a blender container. Add half of the raspberries; cover and blend until mixture is smooth, stirring with a spoon as needed. Transfer mixture to a bowl and repeat blending with remaining beverage and raspberries. Spoon the blended granita into the six orange shells and serve immediately

Serving size: *½ cup*
Calories: *50*
Fat: *0 g*

Variations

- *Omit orange shells and serve granita in small dessert dishes; garnish with a piece of fresh fruit.*
- *Combine tangerine-strawberry soft drink mix, water and 1 (20 oz.) bag of frozen strawberries. Prepare as directed above.*
- *Combine raspberry-lemonade soft drink mix, water and 1 (12 oz.) bag frozen raspberries. Prepare as directed above.*
- *Combine ruby red grapefruit soft drink mix, water and 1 (16 oz.) bag frozen peach slices. Prepare as directed above, but serve in grapefruit shells.*

Fruity Lime Cups

Makes 6 servings

1 (15 oz.) can sliced pears in juice
¼ C. frozen limeade concentrate, thawed
2 tsp. finely grated lime peel
6 sugar-free chewy candy lime slices

Drain pears, reserving ¼ cup of the juice. Place pears, reserved juice, limeade concentrate and lime peel in a blender and puree until smooth. Spoon mixture into six 3-ounce plastic drinking cups. Cover and freeze until firm. Remove from freezer 10 to 15 minutes before serving. Cut a slit into each lime candy slice and place a candy on edge of each cup before serving.

Serving size: *1 (3 oz.) cup*
Calories: *83*
Fat: *0 g*

Variation

• *Turn this dessert into popsicles by spooning mixture into popsicle molds or paper cups. (If using cups, insert wooden sticks into the semi-frozen pops after 90 minutes.) To serve, remove popsicles from molds or tear off paper cups.*

Striped Summer Fruit Pops

Makes 12 servings

2 C. sliced strawberries
¾ C. honey, divided
6 kiwifruit, peeled and sliced
1⅓ C. sliced ripe peaches

In a blender container or food processor, combine strawberries and ¼ cup honey. Cover and blend until mixture is smooth. Divide among twelve (3-ounce) disposable plastic cups or popsicle molds. Freeze for 30 minutes or until firm. In a blender container or food processor, combine kiwifruit and ¼ cup honey. Cover and blend until mixture is smooth. Pour a portion of kiwifruit mixture over frozen strawberry layer in each cup. Insert a wooden stick in each cup. Freeze until firm. Blend peaches with remaining ¼ cup honey in the same manner. Pour a portion of peach mixture over kiwifruit layer. Freeze until firm. Remove from freezer at least 5 minutes before serving. Remove from cups before eating.

Serving size: *1 popsicle*
Calories: *104*
Fat: *0 g*

Lemon Mousse Freeze

¼ C. fresh lemon juice
4 egg yolks
5 T. sugar
¼ C. light butter, chilled and cut into pieces
1½ C. fat-free whipped topping

Place six paper liners into a muffin tin; set aside. In a small heavy saucepan over medium-low heat, combine lemon juice, egg yolks and sugar. Cook, stirring constantly, until mixture thickens, about 5 to 6 minutes. Remove from heat and pour through a fine strainer into a large bowl to remove any lumps. Add butter and stir until melted. Cover with plastic wrap, pressing plastic against the surface of the mixture. Refrigerate for 30 minutes or until chilled. Fold whipped topping into chilled lemon mixture until well combined. Divide mixture among paper-lined cups, swirling the mounds lightly on top. Freeze for 2 hours before serving.

Serving size: *1 dessert cup*
Calories: *149*
Fat: *9 g*

Strawberry Frozen Yogurt

Makes 6 servings

4 C. fresh strawberries, hulled and halved
⅓ C. sugar
2 T. orange juice
½ C. fat-free plain yogurt

Place strawberries in a food processor and blend until smooth, scraping down the sides as needed. Add sugar and orange juice; process for a few seconds until well blended. Add yogurt and pulse several times until blended. Transfer mixture to a bowl; cover and refrigerate until chilled, at least 1 hour or overnight. Pour strawberry mixture into the container of an ice cream maker and process according to manufacturer's instructions. Serve immediately in chilled dishes or transfer to an airtight container and let mixture harden in freezer for 1 to 1½ hours before serving. This may be frozen for up to one week. Let soften in refrigerator for ½ hour before serving.

Serving size: *½ cup*
Calories: *90*
Fat: *trace fat*

Frozen Chocolate Mousse

Makes 9 servings

9 (2½") squares chocolate or honey graham crackers
1¼ C. skim milk
¼ tsp. mint flavoring
2 (1.5 oz.) env. sugar-free, low-fat chocolate mousse mix
1 C. miniature marshmallows
Fresh mint leaves, optional
Fresh blueberries, optional

Line an 8" square baking pan with foil, letting foil extend 2" over ends. Arrange crackers over bottom, cutting to fit. In a large mixing bowl, stir together milk and mint flavoring. Add mousse mix and beat with an electric mixer at low speed until mix is blended. Increase to high speed and beat for about 5 minutes, scraping sides of bowl often. Spoon 1 cup prepared mousse over crackers in pan. Sprinkle marshmallows evenly over mousse and spread with remaining mousse. Cover and freeze for at least 8 hours. Lift foil by the ends and transfer dessert to a cutting board; let stand for 5 to 10 minutes. Cut dessert into nine squares and remove foil before serving. Garnish each piece with mint and blueberries, if desired.

Serving size: *1 piece*
Calories: *85*
Fat: *2.7 g*

Variations

- *Omit marshmallows and crackers. Using a 1½ to 2" round cookie cutter, cut dessert into round pieces. Sprinkle dessert tops with shaved chocolate and garnish each piece with mint leaves and blueberries before serving.*
- *Use crushed crackers in place of whole crackers. Assemble individual desserts in small plastic or paper cups. Freeze as directed. Serve in the cups or unmold desserts to serve on small plates.*

Cookies & Candy

Sugar Cookies

Makes 36 cookies

2½ C. flour
1 tsp. baking powder
Pinch of salt
¾ C. butter, softened
¾ C. sugar
2 eggs
1 T. lemon juice
1 tsp. vanilla extract

In a medium bowl, combine flour, baking powder and salt; set aside. In a large mixing bowl, combine butter and sugar. Beat with an electric mixer at medium-high speed, scraping bowl often, for 2 minutes or until mixture is creamy. Add eggs and beat until fluffy, about 2 to 3 minutes. Add lemon juice and vanilla. Reduce speed to low and slowly add the flour mixture, mixing until blended. Divide dough in half and flatten each portion into a 1" thick disk. Wrap in plastic and refrigerate for at least 1 hour. Preheat oven to 350°. Cover baking sheets with parchment paper. Roll out one portion of dough to ¼" thickness. Cut into desired shapes and place on prepared baking sheet. Combine scraps and roll out again; cut into shapes. Bake cookies for 10 to 15 minutes or until light golden brown.

Serving size: *1 cookie*
Calories: *86*
Fat: *4 g*

Shame-Free

- *Sprinkle tops of cookies with sugar-free fruit-flavored gelatin before baking.*
- *To save 180 calories in this entire recipe, use ½ cup granulated sugar plus a sugar substitute such as Sweet One or Sweet 'N Low equal to ¼ cup sugar.*

Bite-Size Chocolate Mint Meringues

Makes about 60 cookies

3 large egg whites, room temperature

¼ tsp. cream of tartar

⅔ C. sugar

¼ C. unsweetened cocoa powder, sifted

¼ tsp. mint extract

⅓ C. semi-sweet chocolate chips, finely chopped

¼ C. vanilla or white baking chips

¼ C. semi-sweet chocolate chips

2 tsp. shortening, divided

Position oven racks to divide the oven in thirds for even baking. Preheat oven to 300°. Line two baking sheets with parchment paper; set aside. In a large mixing bowl, combine egg whites and cream of tartar. Beat with an electric mixer on medium speed until soft peaks form. Gradually add sugar, one tablespoon at a time, and beat at high speed. Add cocoa powder and continue to beat until mixture becomes glossy and stiff peaks form. Add mint extract. Gently fold in chopped chocolate chips. Spoon small rounds of meringue onto the parchment paper, leaving 1" to 2" between cookies. (Mixture may also be piped.) Bake for 30 minutes or until meringues feel firm, rotating pans halfway through baking. Place baking sheets on a cooling rack for 10 to 15 minutes before peeling cookies off parchment. Meanwhile, place white chips and ¼ cup chocolate chips into two separate small microwave-safe bowls. Add 1 teaspoon of shortening to each bowl and microwave on high power for 20 to 30 seconds or until melted. Stir until smooth. Drizzle over meringue cookies as desired. Store in an airtight container for up to 2 weeks.

Serving size: *2 cookies*
Calories: *48*
Fat: *0.3 g*

Apricot Cookie Strips

¼ C. brown sugar

2 T. shortening

2 T. butter, softened

½ tsp. vanilla extract

1 egg yolk

1½ C. biscuit baking mix

⅓ C. apricot fruit spread, no sugar added

½ C. powdered sugar

1 to 1½ T. skim milk

Preheat oven to 350°. In a medium bowl, combine brown sugar, shortening, butter, vanilla and egg yolk until well blended. Stir in baking mix. Divide dough into four equal parts. Shape each portion into an 8 x 1" strip and place crosswise on ungreased baking sheet. With the handle of a wooden spoon, make a slight indentation lengthwise down the center of each strip. Fill each indentation with 1½ tablespoons of fruit spread. Bake 12 to 14 minutes or until edges are light brown. Cool slightly on baking sheet. Meanwhile, in a small bowl, mix powdered sugar and enough milk to make a smooth glaze, thin enough to drizzle. Drizzle glaze over tops of cookie strips. Cut each strip diagonally into 1" pieces.

Serving size: *2 cookies*
Calories: *120*
Fat: *5 g*

Variation

- *Use different fruit spreads, such as raspberry, strawberry or orange marmalade.*

Coconut Balls

4 large egg whites, room temperature
Dash of cream of tartar
¼ tsp. salt
⅔ C. sugar
1 tsp. vanilla extract
¼ C. flour
3 C. sweetened flaked coconut

Preheat oven to 325°. Grease two baking sheets with nonstick cooking spray; set aside. In a medium mixing bowl, beat together egg whites and cream of tartar with an electric mixer at medium-high speed until stiff peaks form. Beat in salt, sugar, vanilla and flour. Stir in coconut. Drop batter by rounded teaspoonfuls, 1" apart, on prepared baking sheets. Bake for 20 to 25 minutes or until lightly browned. Let cookies cool several minutes on baking sheets, then transfer cookies to wire racks to cool completely.

Serving size: *1 cookie*
Calories: *78*
Fat: *3 g*

Shame-Free

To enjoy the flavor of coconut without the calories, use unsweetened flaked coconut. Make powdered coconut to sprinkle over cakes, candies or fruit compotes. Just place 1¼ cups coconut in a food processor and process until it looks like powdered sugar.

Sliced Cappuccino Rounds

Makes 56 cookies

1 T. instant coffee granules

2 C. flour

1 tsp. ground cinnamon

¼ tsp. salt

½ C. plus 3 T. shortening, divided

½ C. butter, softened

½ C. sugar

½ C. brown sugar

2 (1 oz.) squares unsweetened chocolate, melted

1 egg

1½ C. semi-sweet chocolate chips

In a custard cup, dissolve coffee granules in 1 teaspoon water; set aside. In a medium bowl, stir together flour, cinnamon and salt; set aside. In a large mixing bowl, use an electric mixer to cream together ½ cup shortening, butter, sugar and brown sugar at medium speed until light and fluffy. Beat in coffee mixture, melted chocolate and egg. Stir in the flour mixture until well blended. Cover bowl and chill for 1 hour or until dough is no longer sticky. Shape dough into two rolls, each about 7" long. Wrap tightly in plastic and chill for 6 or more hours. When ready to bake cookies, preheat oven to 350°. Cut rolls of dough into ¼" thick slices. Place slices on ungreased baking sheets and bake for 10 to 12 minutes. Transfer cookies to wire racks to cool. Meanwhile, in a small saucepan over low heat, melt chocolate chips and 3 tablespoons shortening, stirring occasionally until smooth. Remove from heat. Dip half of each cookie into chocolate mixture and place on waxed paper until chocolate is set.

Serving size: 1 cookie
Calories: 100
Fat: 6 g

Chocolate Drops

Makes 36 cookies

1¾ C. flour
½ C. unsweetened cocoa powder
1 tsp. baking powder
½ tsp. baking soda
1 (1 oz.) square unsweetened chocolate, chopped
3 T. vegetable oil
4 egg whites
1 egg
1 C. sugar
½ C. brown sugar
¼ C. pureed prunes *(directions on page 5)*
2 T. light corn syrup
1 tsp. vanilla extract
¼ C. miniature semi-sweet chocolate chips

Preheat oven to 350°. Coat two baking sheets with nonstick cooking spray; set aside. In a medium bowl, stir together flour, cocoa powder, baking powder and baking soda; set aside. In a microwave-safe bowl, heat chocolate and oil on high power for 40 to 60 seconds, stirring until melted and smooth; let cool slightly. In a separate large mixing bowl, combine egg whites, egg, sugar and brown sugar. Beat on high speed for 3 to 5 minutes. Reduce mixer speed to low and beat in melted chocolate mixture, prunes, corn syrup and vanilla. Beat for 1 minute. Stir in flour mixture. Fold in chocolate chips. Drop batter on prepared baking sheets by tablespoonfuls, leaving about 2″ between cookies. Bake for 11 to 13 minutes or until centers begin to set. Cool for 2 minutes on baking sheets before removing to wire racks to cool completely.

Serving size: *1 cookie*
Calories: *88*
Fat: *2.2 g*

Peanut Butter Cookies

Makes 36 cookies

1¼ C. flour

1 tsp. baking powder

½ C. margarine, softened

½ C. plus 4 tsp. sugar, divided

½ C. peanut butter

1 egg

1 tsp. vanilla extract

In a small bowl, whisk together flour and baking powder; set aside. In a large mixing bowl, beat margarine at medium speed until smooth. Add ½ cup sugar, peanut butter, egg and vanilla; beat for 1 minute. Slowly add the flour mixture and beat just until combined, about 1 minute. The dough will be crumbly; cover and chill for 30 minutes. Before baking, preheat oven to 350°. Line two baking sheets with parchment paper. Place 4 teaspoons sugar into a small shallow bowl. Remove chilled dough from refrigerator and roll it into 1" balls. Dip top of each cookie ball into sugar and place balls, sugar side up, 2" apart on prepared baking sheets. Flatten top of each cookie with a fork, making a criss-cross pattern, so each cookie is about ½" thick. Bake for 7 to 9 minutes or until firm. Gently remove cookies to a wire rack to cool.

Serving size: *1 cookie*
Calories: *77*
Fat: *4.7 g*

Lemon Cookies

Makes 24 cookies

1 C. plus 1 T. flour
3 T. sugar substitute
4 T. powdered sugar, divided
1½ T. grated lemon peel
1 tsp. baking powder
¼ C. margarine
1 egg, beaten
1 T. lemon juice

In a food processor, combine flour, sugar substitute, 3 tablespoons powdered sugar, lemon peel and baking powder. Add the margarine and pulse on and off until coarse crumbs form. Add egg and lemon juice; process until mixture forms into a dough. Remove dough from processor and shape it into a ball. Wrap dough in plastic wrap and refrigerate for at least 1 hour or until firm. When ready to bake, preheat oven to 350°. Coat a baking sheet with nonstick cooking spray. Shape dough into 1" balls and place them 1" apart on prepared baking sheet. Bake for 10 minutes or until cookies are golden. Remove cookies from baking sheet and dust with remaining 1 tablespoon powdered sugar. Cool on wire rack.

Serving size: *2 cookies*
Calories: *100*
Fat: *4 g*

Variation

• *Glaze tops of baked cookies with a thin mixture of lemon juice and powdered sugar (though this will add a few calories).*

Lemon Fudge

Makes 2 pounds

6 T. butter, divided

2 (10 to 12 oz.) pkgs. vanilla or white baking chips

⅔ C. sweetened condensed milk

⅔ C. marshmallow creme

1½ tsp. lemon extract

Line a 9" square baking pan with foil, leaving several inches hanging over on opposite sides. Grease foil with butter or butter-flavored nonstick cooking spray; set aside. In a large saucepan over low heat, melt butter. Add chips and sweetened condensed milk, cooking and stirring for 10 to 12 minutes or until chips are melted. Stir in marshmallow creme and lemon extract. Cook and stir 3 to 4 minutes longer or until mixture is smooth and well blended. Pour into prepared pan and chill until set. Using foil, lift fudge out of pan. Discard foil; cut fudge into 64 small squares. If desired, place each square into a miniature paper liner and set on a serving plate with a variety of candies.

Serving size: *1 piece*
Calories: *72*
Fat: *4 g*

Nutty Lemon Chocolate Truffles

5 oz. dark chocolate
¼ C. 2% milk
9 oz. low-fat cream cheese
½ C. chopped dried cranberries
¼ C. finely chopped toasted walnuts*
¾ C. finely chopped pecans
1 tsp. grated lemon peel
1 tsp. ground cinnamon or allspice, optional
3 T. unsweetened cocoa powder

In a small saucepan over low heat, combine chocolate and milk until chocolate is melted, stirring constantly. Remove from heat and allow mixture to cool slightly. In a medium bowl, beat cream cheese until smooth. Add chocolate mixture, cranberries, walnuts, pecans, lemon peel and allspice; mix well. Pour cocoa powder onto a plate. Shape rounded tablespoonfuls of mixture into balls and lightly roll each one in cocoa powder to coat. Place balls in miniature paper liner cups and chill until ready to serve.

To toast, place walnuts in a single layer on a baking sheet. Bake at 350° for approximately 10 minutes or until walnuts are golden brown.

Serving size: *1 truffle*
Calories: *87*
Fat: *5.5 g*

Mock Chocolate Rum Truffles

Makes 42 candies

3 eggs

1 tsp. rum extract

1 T. frozen orange juice concentrate, thawed

Powdered sugar substitute equal to 1 C. sugar

⅓ C. unsweetened cocoa powder

1⅓ C. very fine dry bread crumbs

In a medium mixing bowl, use an electric mixer on medium speed to beat together eggs, rum extract, orange juice concentrate and ¼ cup water until thick and lemon-colored, about 5 to 7 minutes. Gradually add sugar substitute and mix until well blended. Fold in cocoa powder and bread crumbs. Mixture will become very dense. Shape rounded teaspoonfuls of mixture into small balls. Let stand at room temperature until the outsides are dry to the touch. Store in an airtight container in refrigerator.

Serving size: 3 truffles
Calories: 73
Fat: 2 g

Almond Date Kisses

Makes 25 cookies

⅓ C. sliced almonds

1 large egg white, room temperature

Pinch of salt

⅛ tsp. cream of tartar

¼ tsp. rum extract

2 T. sugar

3 T. brown sugar

½ C. chopped dates

½ C. chopped raisins

Position oven racks to divide the oven in thirds for even baking. Preheat oven to 300°. Cover two baking sheets with parchment paper and spray with nonstick cooking spray; set aside. In a non-stick skillet over medium-high heat, toast almonds until lightly browned, about 15 minutes, stirring several times; set aside to cool. In a small mixing bowl, use an electric mixer at medium speed to beat together egg white, salt and cream of tartar until soft peaks form. Add rum extract. Continue to beat, gradually adding sugar and then brown sugar, one tablespoon at a time. Fold in dates, raisins and toasted almonds. Drop mixture by teaspoonfuls onto prepared baking sheets, 3″ apart. Bake for 20 minutes or until light brown, firm and dry to the touch, rotating pans halfway through baking time. Turn off oven and let cookies rest in oven for 20 minutes. Remove pans from oven and cool completely on baking sheets before removing. Serve immediately or store in an airtight container with waxed paper between layers for up to 3 days.

Serving size: *2 cookies*
Calories: *74*
Fat: *2 g*

Peanut-Cereal Treats

Makes 18 pieces

3 C. crisp rice and corn cereal squares
½ C. salted peanuts
⅓ C. brown sugar
⅓ C. corn syrup
¼ C. peanut butter

In a medium bowl, combine cereal and peanuts; set aside. In a microwave-safe bowl, combine brown sugar and corn syrup. Cook on high power for 30 to 60 seconds or until sugar dissolves, stirring several times. Stir in peanut butter until smooth. Pour mixture over cereal and peanuts in bowl; toss to coat well. Drop by rounded tablespoonfuls onto waxed paper. Cool.

Serving size: 1 piece
Calories: 95
Fat: 4 g

How-to Tip

Purchase pure vanilla rather than imitation vanillin, which can have a slightly bitter taste. Almond extract tends to be very strong so use less of it than other extracts and flavorings.

Bars & Cakes

Swirled Pumpkin-Carrot Bars

Makes 48 bars

4 oz. light cream cheese or Neufchâtel, softened

1¼ C. sugar, divided

1 T. milk

2 C. flour

2¼ tsp. pumpkin pie spice

2 tsp. baking powder

1 tsp. baking soda

⅓ C. butter, softened

½ C. brown sugar

2 eggs

2 egg whites

1 (15 oz.) can pumpkin puree

1 C. finely shredded carrot

Preheat oven to 350°. Spray a 10 x 15" jellyroll pan with nonstick cooking spray; set aside. In a small mixing bowl, beat together cream cheese, ¼ cup sugar and milk with an electric mixer at medium-low speed until creamy and well blended; set aside. In a small bowl, combine flour, pumpkin pie spice, baking powder and baking soda; set aside. In a large mixing bowl, beat together remaining 1 cup sugar, butter and brown sugar on medium-low speed until crumbly. Add eggs, egg whites, pumpkin and carrot; beat until well blended. Add flour mixture and beat well. Spread batter evenly in prepared pan. Drop teaspoonfuls of the cream cheese mixture over batter; swirl with a knife. Bake for 25 to 30 minutes or until a toothpick inserted near center comes out clean. Cool bars in pan.

Serving size: *1 bar*
Calories: *75*
Fat: *1.7 g*

Banana Bars

½ C. Fiber One bran cereal
⅔ C. sugar
½ C. low-fat sour cream
2 T. butter, softened
2 egg whites
¾ C. mashed ripe banana
1 tsp. vanilla extract
1 C. flour
½ tsp. baking soda
¼ tsp. salt
Powdered sugar, optional

Preheat oven to 375°. Coat a 9" square baking pan with nonstick cooking spray; set aside. Crush cereal with a rolling pin; set aside. In a large mixing bowl, use an electric mixer to beat together sugar, sour cream, butter and egg whites at low speed for 1 minute, scraping bowl occasionally. Add banana and vanilla, beat well for 30 seconds. Beat in flour, baking soda and salt at medium speed for 1 minute or until well blended, scraping bowl. Stir in crushed cereal. Spread batter in prepared pan. Bake for 20 to 25 minutes or until light brown; cool. Sprinkle with powdered sugar before serving, if desired.

Serving size: *1 bar*
Calories: *70*
Fat: *1.6 g*

Raspberry Lemon Bars

Makes 20 bars

¾ C. plus 2 T. flour, divided

2 C. granulated Splenda, divided

Pinch of salt

¼ C. light butter (40% fat)

½ C. egg substitute

½ C. half-and-half

½ C. lemon juice

1 T. grated lemon peel

¼ C. reduced-sugar raspberry preserves

Preheat oven to 350°. Coat an 8" square baking pan with butter-flavored nonstick cooking spray; set aside. To make crust, mix together ¾ cup flour, ¾ cup Splenda granular and salt in a medium bowl. With a pastry blender or two knives, cut in butter until mixture is crumbly. Do not over-mix. Press dough into prepared baking pan. Bake for 15 to 20 minutes or until lightly browned. Meanwhile, make filling by combining remaining 1¼ cups Splenda granular and remaining 2 tablespoons flour in a medium bowl; stir well. Add egg substitute and half-and-half; stir until well blended. Slowly add lemon juice while stirring constantly. Stir in lemon peel; set aside. Break up raspberry preserves with a spoon. When crust is baked, spread preserves over warm crust. Gently pour lemon mixture over preserves. Bake for 20 to 25 minutes or until set. Remove from oven and allow to cool. Place pan into refrigerator and chill for 2 hours before cutting.

Serving size: *1 bar*
Calories: *59*
Fat: *2.4 g*

Mocha Brownies

Makes 12 bars

½ C. flour

½ C. unsweetened cocoa powder

½ tsp. baking powder

¼ C. light margarine (40% fat)

1 T. instant coffee granules

1 C. sugar

2 eggs or egg substitute equal to 2 eggs

¼ C. pureed prunes *(directions on page 5)*

2 tsp. vanilla extract

2 T. powdered sugar

Preheat oven to 350°. Coat an 8" square baking pan with nonstick cooking spray; set aside. In a small bowl, combine flour, cocoa powder and baking powder; mix well and set aside. In a medium saucepan over medium-low heat, melt margarine. Add coffee granules and stir until dissolved. Remove from heat and let mixture cool slightly. Add sugar, egg substitute, prunes and vanilla to coffee mixture; stir well until combined. Fold cocoa mixture into sugar mixture until well mixed. Spoon batter into prepared baking pan. Bake for 18 to 20 minutes or until a toothpick inserted near center comes out almost clean. (A few fudge crumbs should cling to it.) Cool brownies in the pan. Then sift powdered sugar evenly over brownies.

Serving size: *1 brownie*
Calories: *135*
Fat: *3.3 g*

Chocolate Chip Almond Bars

Makes 25 bars

½ C. sugar

½ C. plus 1 T. butter, softened, divided

2 tsp. almond extract

1 egg

1 C. flour

½ tsp. baking powder

¼ tsp. salt

½ C. semi-sweet chocolate chips

½ C. powdered sugar

1 T. skim milk

⅓ C. sliced almonds

Preheat oven to 350°. Coat an 8" square baking pan with nonstick cooking spray; set aside. In a large mixing bowl, combine sugar, ½ cup butter and almond extract. With an electric mixer, beat at medium speed until creamy, scraping bowl often. Add egg and mix well. Reduce speed to low; add flour, baking powder and salt. Beat until well mixed, scraping bowl often. Stir in chocolate chips with a spoon. Spread batter into prepared pan. Bake for 25 to 30 minutes or until edges are golden brown. Cool completely in pan. To make glaze, combine powdered sugar, remaining 1 tablespoon butter and milk in a small bowl, beating well until smooth. Spread over cooled bars. Sprinkle almonds over top, pressing them lightly into glaze.

Serving size: *1 bar*
Calories: *115*
Fat: *6.4 g*

Tropical Lime Bars

Makes 16 bars

35 reduced-fat vanilla
  wafers
3 T. powdered sugar,
  divided
2 T. sweetened flaked
  coconut
2 T. light butter
3 large egg whites
2 eggs

1½ C. sugar (or 1 C. sugar
  plus ½ C. granulated
  sugar substitute)
3 T. flour
1 tsp. baking powder
1½ tsp. grated lime peel
½ C. lime juice
Additional grated lime
  peel, optional

Preheat oven to 350°. Line a 9" square baking pan with foil and coat with nonstick cooking spray; set aside. In a food processor, pulse wafers, 2 tablespoons powdered sugar and coconut until wafers are reduced to fine crumbs. Add butter and pulse until mixture is damp. Press crumb mixture firmly into bottom of prepared pan. Bake for 10 minutes or until crust is pale golden brown and set. Meanwhile, in a medium bowl, whisk together egg whites, eggs and sugar until thick and well blended. Add flour, baking powder, lime peel and lime juice; whisk until mixed. Pour filling over hot crust and return to oven; bake for 30 additional minutes or until topping is pale golden brown and just set. Remove pan to cool on a wire rack. Immediately loosen edges with tip of knife where topping meets foil. Cool completely, then refrigerate for 1 hour. To serve, lift bars from pan by the foil and transfer to a cutting board. Remove foil and cut into squares. Dust with remaining 1 tablespoon powdered sugar and top with additional lime peel, if desired.

Serving size: *1 bar*
Calories: *150*
Fat: *2.8 g*

Blueberry-Lemon Squares

Makes 36 bars

2 C. plus 3 T. flour, divided

½ C. powdered sugar

2 T. cornstarch

¼ tsp. salt

¾ C. butter

4 eggs, lightly beaten

1½ C. sugar (or 1 C. sugar plus ½ C. granulated sugar substitute)

1 tsp. finely grated lemon peel

¾ C. lemon juice

¼ C. fat-free half-and-half

1½ C. fresh blueberries

Preheat oven to 350°. Line a 9 x 13" baking pan with foil, extending foil over ends of pan. Coat foil with nonstick cooking spray; set aside. In a large mixing bowl, combine 2 cups flour, powdered sugar, cornstarch and salt. Using a pastry blender or two knives, cut in butter until mixture resembles coarse crumbs. Press mixture into bottom of prepared pan. Bake for 18 to 20 minutes or until edges are golden. Meanwhile, in a medium bowl, stir together eggs, sugar, remaining 3 tablespoons flour, lemon peel, lemon juice and half-and-half until well blended. Pour filling over hot partially baked crust. Sprinkle blueberries evenly over filling. Bake for 20 to 25 minutes more or until center is set. Cool completely in pan. Grasp foil overhang and lift from pan. Remove foil and cut into bars. Cover and store in refrigerator for up to 3 days.

Serving size: *1 bar*
Calories: *117*
Fat: *4.5 g*

Lime-Coconut Bars

Makes 36 bars

1 C. lime juice
2 (14 oz.) cans fat-free sweetened condensed milk
1 tsp. finely grated lime peel
2 drops green food coloring
1½ C. flour
½ C. sugar
½ C. finely chopped slivered almonds
½ C. butter
½ C. sweetened flaked coconut

Preheat oven to 350°. In a large bowl, whisk together lime juice, sweetened condensed milk, lime peel and food coloring; set filling mixture aside. In another large bowl, combine flour, sugar and chopped almonds. Using a pastry blender or two knives, cut in butter until mixture resembles coarse crumbs. Pat mixture into an ungreased 9 x 13" baking pan. Bake for 16 to 18 minutes or until edges are lightly browned. Pour filling mixture over hot, partially baked crust. Sprinkle with coconut. Bake for 15 to 17 minutes longer or until filling is set. Cool completely in pan. Cut into bars. Cover and store in refrigerator.

> **Serving size:** *1 bar*
> **Calories:** *130*
> **Fat:** *2.3 g*

Lemon Pudding Cake

Makes 4 servings

2 eggs, separated
⅛ tsp. cream of tartar
¾ C. skim milk
3 T. whole wheat pastry flour
¼ C. lemon juice
⅛ tsp. baking soda
2 T. honey
1 T. butter, melted
1 tsp. grated lemon peel
½ tsp. lemon extract

Preheat oven to 350°. Lightly butter a 1½-quart casserole dish; set aside. In a medium mixing bowl, use an electric mixer to beat egg whites until foamy. Add cream of tartar and continue beating until stiff peaks form; set aside. In a separate large bowl, beat egg yolks; set aside. In a jar with a tight-fitting lid, combine milk and flour; shake vigorously. Beat milk mixture into egg yolks. Add lemon juice, baking soda, honey, butter, lemon peel and lemon extract; blend together well. Stir a small amount of the yolk mixture into whites; then fold whites into yolk mixture. Turn into prepared dish and set dish in a pan of hot water on the bottom rack of oven. Bake for 55 to 60 minutes. Serve warm in dessert bowls.

Serving size: *¼ of dish*
Calories: *136*
Fat: *5.6 g*

Citrus-Filled Angel Food Cake

Makes 14 servings

1 (1 oz.) pkg. sugar-free, fat-free instant lemon pudding mix
1½ C. skim milk
1 T. orange juice
1 tsp. grated orange peel
½ tsp. orange extract
1 (10") prepared angel food cake
1 C. sugar-free, fat-free whipped topping

In a medium bowl, combine pudding mix, milk, juice, orange peel and orange extract, mixing well until pudding thickens. Cover bowl and chill until set, about 30 minutes. To put dessert together, slice angel food cake horizontally into three layers. Fold whipped topping into pudding mixture. Spread a third of the pudding mixture on top of bottom cake layer. Set middle cake layer on top of pudding mixture. Spread another third of pudding mixture on top of this cake layer and stack final cake layer on top. Spread remaining pudding mixture on top layer of cake. Chill for 1 hour before serving.

Serving size: *1 slice*
Calories: *146*
Fat: *0.1 g*

Shame-Free

When preparing a fluffy frosting recipe, reduce the calories by substituting marshmallow creme for the butter or margarine.

Pumpkin Angel Cake

Makes 14 servings

1 C. canned pumpkin puree

1 tsp. vanilla extract

½ tsp. ground cinnamon

½ tsp. ground nutmeg

¼ tsp. ground cloves

⅛ tsp. ground ginger

1 (16 oz.) pkg. angel food cake mix

1 C. sugar-free, fat-free whipped topping

Additional ground cinnamon, optional

Remove upper rack from oven. Preheat oven to 350°. In a large bowl, combine pumpkin, vanilla, cinnamon, nutmeg, cloves and ginger. Prepare cake mix according to package directions. Fold ¼ of the cake batter into pumpkin mixture; gently fold in the remaining batter. Spoon mixture into an ungreased 10″ tube pan. Cut through batter with a knife to remove air pockets. Bake on lowest rack in oven for 38 to 44 minutes or until the top is golden brown, cake springs back when lightly touched and entire top appears dry. Immediately invert pan and cool cake completely, about 1 hour. Run a knife around side and center tube of pan. Remove cake to a serving plate. Slice cake and garnish each serving with about 1 tablespoon whipped topping. Sprinkle with a dash of cinnamon, if desired.

Serving size: *1 slice*
Calories: *135*
Fat: *trace fat*

Carrot Cake

¼ C. apple butter
¼ C. vegetable oil
1 egg
2 tsp. vanilla extract
1¼ C. flour
¾ C. Equal Sugar Lite
1 tsp. baking soda
1 tsp. ground cinnamon
¼ tsp. salt
1 C. shredded carrot
¼ C. raisins
¼ C. well drained, crushed pineapple
2 T. powdered sugar

Preheat oven to 350°. Coat an 8" square baking pan with nonstick cooking spray; set aside. In a large mixing bowl, combine apple butter, oil, egg and vanilla; beat at medium speed with an electric mixer until well blended. In a separate bowl, stir together flour, sugar substitute, baking soda, cinnamon and salt. Add flour mixture to mixing bowl and beat at low speed until well combined. Fold in carrot, raisins and pineapple just until blended. Spread batter in prepared pan and bake for 30 to 35 minutes or until a toothpick inserted near center comes out clean. Cool cake completely in pan. Cut cake into 12 pieces and sprinkle each piece with powdered sugar before serving.

Serving size: *1 piece*
Calories: *136*
Fat: *5.2 g*

Rhubarb Cake

Makes 20 servings

1¼ C. flour
¾ C. whole wheat flour
1 tsp. baking powder
½ tsp. baking soda
2 tsp. ground cinnamon, divided
¼ tsp salt
½ C. light margarine, softened (40% fat)

¾ C. brown sugar, divided
½ C. sugar
1 egg
1 tsp. vanilla extract
1 C. low-fat buttermilk
2 C. finely diced rhubarb
⅓ C. walnuts, chopped

Preheat oven to 350°. Coat a 9 x 13" baking pan with nonstick cooking spray; set aside. In medium bowl, stir together flour, whole wheat flour, baking powder, baking soda, ¼ teaspoon cinnamon and salt; set aside. In a large mixing bowl, cream together margarine, ½ cup brown sugar and sugar on medium speed. Add egg and vanilla, beating until mixture is fluffy. To this mixture, alternately add flour mixture and buttermilk, ending with dry ingredients. Beat until well combined. Stir in rhubarb; pour batter into prepared pan. In a small bowl, mix together remaining ¼ cup brown sugar, 1½ teaspoons cinnamon and walnuts. Sprinkle topping mixture evenly over batter in pan. Bake for 35 to 40 minutes or until a toothpick inserted in center of cake comes out clean. Cool before cutting.

Serving size: *1 piece*
Calories: *136*
Fat: *4.2 g*

Guest-Worthy Desserts

Crunchy Apple Crisp

½ C. uncooked oats

6 C. thinly sliced baking apples

½ C. frozen apple juice concentrate, thawed

1 tsp. ground cinnamon

¼ tsp. ground cloves

2 T. raisins or dried sweetened cranberries, optional

⅓ C. Grape Nuts or other crunchy cereal

Sugar-free, fat-free whipped topping

Preheat oven to 350°. Spray an 8" square baking pan with nonstick cooking spray. Spread oats in the bottom of prepared pan. Arrange the apple slices evenly over oats. In a small bowl, combine apple juice concentrate, cinnamon and cloves; pour mixture over apples and oats. Sprinkle raisins or cranberries on top, if desired. Cover pan with foil and bake for 1 hour. Remove foil and sprinkle cereal on top of apples. Bake for an additional 10 minutes. Serve with a small dollop of whipped topping.

Serving size: *about ¾ cup*
Calories: *150*
Fat: *0.7 g*

Apple Soufflé

3 medium baking apples, peeled, cored and cut
   into 1" pieces
3 T. sugar substitute such as granulated Splenda
½ tsp. almond extract
5 egg whites, room temperature
¼ tsp. cream of tartar
¼ C. sliced almonds, toasted*

In a medium saucepan over high heat, combine apple pieces with ¼ cup water. Bring to a boil. Reduce heat to low, cover and simmer for 10 minutes or until apples are tender, stirring occasionally. Stir in sugar substitute and almond extract. Remove from heat and refrigerate for 10 minutes, placing pan on a hot pad. Preheat oven to 425°. In a large mixing bowl, use an electric mixer at high speed to beat egg whites and cream of tartar until stiff peaks form. Use a rubber scraper to gently fold beaten egg whites into cooled apple mixture. Gently spoon mixture into a 1½-quart soufflé dish. Bake for 15 minutes or until puffed and browned. Sprinkle with almonds before serving. Serve warm.

* To toast, place almonds in a single layer on a baking sheet. Bake at 350° for approximately 10 minutes or until almonds are golden brown.

Serving size: *¼ of dish*
Calories: *120*
Fat: *6.3 g*

Layered
Strawberry Squares

Makes 6 servings

2 (0.3 oz.) pkgs. sugar-free strawberry gelatin powder
1½ C. light whipped topping, divided
Fresh strawberries with hulls, optional

In a large microwave-safe bowl, bring 1½ cups water to a boil. Add gelatin and stir for 2 minutes or until gelatin is completely dissolved. In a large measuring cup, combine 1 cup cold water and enough ice cubes to measure 1½ cups. Add to gelatin and stir until ice is completely melted. Remove 1½ cups of gelatin and set aside. Refrigerate remaining gelatin for 20 to 30 minutes or until slightly thickened. After 30 minutes, add ¾ cup of whipped topping to cooled, thickened gelatin and whisk together until well blended. Pour mixture into an 8" square glass dish. Refrigerate for 15 minutes or until gelatin mixture is set but not firm. Carefully pour reserved gelatin over creamy layer in dish. Refrigerate for 3 hours or until firm. Cut into squares and serve with a dollop of remaining ¾ cup whipped topping and a fanned strawberry* on top.

Serving size: *1 piece*
Calories: *54*
Fat: *0 g*

Variation

• *Make Layered Orange Squares using sugar-free orange gelatin and mandarin orange segments. If desired, substitute frozen orange juice concentrate for the water and ice mixture.*

How-to Tip

* To fan a strawberry, thinly slice berry from pointed end toward hull five times, without cutting through cap. Gently fan cut ends apart.

Raspberry Gelatin Coolies

Makes 6 servings

1 (0.3 oz.) pkg. sugar-free raspberry gelatin powder
1 C. cold orange juice
1 C. fresh raspberries, slightly mashed
Whipped topping, optional
4 whole fresh raspberries, optional

In a microwave-safe bowl, bring 1 cup water to a boil. Add gelatin and stir for 2 minutes or until gelatin is completely dissolved. Stir in orange juice. Refrigerate for 20 to 30 minutes or until gelatin is slightly thickened. Stir in raspberries until well blended. Pour into individual dessert cups and refrigerate 4 hours or until firm. Serve with a dollop of whipped topping and a fresh raspberry on top.

Serving size: *1 dessert dish*
Calories: *69*
Fat: *0.4 g*

Lemon-Berry Trifles

Makes 4 servings

2 C. cubed angel food cake

½ C. sugar-free, fat-free whipped topping

1 C. fat-free lemon yogurt

1 C. mixed berries, such as raspberries, blueberries
   or sliced strawberries

Fresh mint leaves, optional

Divide cake cubes among four glass dessert dishes; set aside. In a small mixing bowl, fold whipped topping into yogurt until well mixed. Spoon yogurt mixture on top of cake in each dish. Sprinkle berries on top. Garnish with mint before serving, if desired.

Serving size: *1 dessert cup*
Calories: *148*
Fat: *0.2 g*

Berry & Cream Stacks

Makes 4 servings

1 T. sugar

½ tsp. ground cinnamon

3 sheets frozen phyllo dough, thawed

½ C. sugar-free, fat-free whipped topping

1 C. sugar-free, fat-free vanilla pudding prepared
with skim milk

1 C. fresh raspberries or 1½ C. sliced strawberries

Powdered sugar

Preheat oven to 350°. In a small bowl, stir together sugar and cinnamon; set aside. Spray one sheet of phyllo dough with butter-flavored nonstick cooking spray. Sprinkle a third of cinnamon-sugar mixture over dough. Place a second sheet of phyllo on top; spray dough and sprinkle another third of sugar mixture on top. Place remaining sheet of phyllo on top, spray and sprinkle with remaining sugar mixture. Use a pizza cutter or sharp knife to cut stacked phyllo into 12 squares. Transfer to a baking sheet and bake for 8 to 10 minutes or until puffed and crisp. Remove from oven and cool completely. Meanwhile, in a small bowl, fold whipped topping into pudding until well blended. To serve, spoon a portion of pudding mixture on four baked pastry squares; top with a few berries. Repeat with a second layer, then top with remaining pastry squares to make four dessert stacks. Dust desserts with powdered sugar.

Serving size: *1 stack*
Calories: *134*
Fat: *1 g*

No-Fuss Lemon Cheesecake

Makes 8 servings

2 T. graham cracker crumbs, divided

1 (0.3 oz.) pkg. sugar-free lemon gelatin powder

1 C. low-fat cottage cheese

1 (8 oz.) tub light cream cheese spread

2 C. light whipped topping

1 C. light cherry pie filling

Generously coat a 9" pie pan with nonstick cooking spray. Sprinkle 1 tablespoon graham cracker crumbs over bottom of pan; set aside. In a small bowl, combine gelatin with ⅔ cup boiling water. Stir for 2 minutes or until completely dissolved. Cool mixture for 5 minutes, then pour into a blender container. Add cottage cheese and cream cheese; blend until smooth, stopping occasionally to scrape down sides of blender. Pour mixture into a large bowl. Gently fold in whipped topping until combined. Pour into prepared pan and sprinkle remaining 1 tablespoon graham cracker crumbs over top. Refrigerate for 4 hours or until firm. Just before serving, top with pie filling. Refrigerate any leftovers.

Serving size: *1 slice*
Calories: *150*
Fat: *7 g*

Orange Dream Cheesecake

Makes 8 servings

2 T. graham cracker crumbs
1 (0.3 oz.) pkg. sugar-free orange gelatin powder
1 C. low-fat cottage cheese
1 (8 oz.) tub fat-free cream cheese spread
2 C. sugar-free, fat-free whipped topping
8 mandarin orange segments, optional

Generously coat the bottom of an 8" or 9" springform pan with nonstick cooking spray. Sprinkle graham cracker crumbs over bottom of pan; set aside. In a small bowl, combine gelatin with ⅔ cup boiling water. Stir for 2 minutes or until completely dissolved. Cool mixture for 5 minutes, then pour into a blender container. Add cottage cheese and cream cheese; blend until smooth, stopping occasionally to scrape down sides of blender. Pour into a large bowl. Gently fold in whipped topping until well combined. Pour mixture into prepared pan and smooth top with a spoon. Refrigerate 4 hours or until set. Remove rim of pan and cut into pieces. Garnish each piece with an orange segment and serve. Refrigerate any leftovers.

Serving size: *1 slice*
Calories: *75*
Fat: *1.5 g*

Chocolate Cheesecake Indulgence

Makes 12 servings

6 (2½") squares chocolate graham crackers, crushed

2⅓ C. part-skim ricotta cheese

4 oz. nonfat cream cheese, softened

½ C. sugar

¼ C. unsweetened cocoa powder

1 egg

3 T. flour

2 T. sugar-free Amaretto syrup or liqueur

1 tsp. vanilla extract

1 T. semi-sweet chocolate chips, grated, optional

Fresh raspberries or strawberries, optional

Preheat oven to 300°. Generously coat an 8" springform pan with nonstick cooking spray. Sprinkle cracker crumbs evenly over the bottom of pan; set aside. In a blender container or food processor, blend together ricotta cheese, cream cheese, sugar, cocoa powder, egg, flour, syrup and vanilla; blend until smooth and well mixed. Pour cheese mixture over crumbs in pan. Bake for about 1½ hours or until a knife inserted in the center comes out clean. Cool completely. Cover and refrigerate until chilled, at least 3 hours. If desired, sprinkle grated chocolate on top and garnish each slice with several fresh berries before serving.

Serving size: 1 slice
Calories: 142
Fat: 5.1 g

Premium Brownie Pie

Makes 8 servings

3 egg whites

2 T. brown sugar

18 (2½") chocolate graham cracker squares, finely crushed

¼ C. finely chopped walnuts

½ tsp. vanilla extract

2 C. nonfat frozen vanilla yogurt, slightly softened

Sliced strawberries, optional

Preheat oven to 325°. Coat a 9" pie pan with nonstick cooking spray; set aside. In a large bowl, use an electric mixer at medium-high speed to beat egg whites until soft peaks form, about 3 to 4 minutes. Gradually add the sugar, beating for 2 to 3 minutes or until stiff peaks form. With a rubber scraper, gently fold in cracker crumbs, walnuts and vanilla until just blended. Transfer mixture into prepared pan, spreading evenly. Bake for 25 minutes or until firm and a toothpick inserted in center comes out clean. Cool completely on a wire rack. Spread softened frozen yogurt over brownie pie; cover and freeze for 2 to 3 hours or until yogurt is very firm. Slice into wedges and garnish with a few sliced strawberries, if desired.

Serving size: *1 wedge*
Calories: *135*
Fat: *3.1 g*

Lemon-Raspberry Custard Cakes

Makes 8 servings

1 C. raspberries, divided

4 eggs

¾ C. sugar, divided

2 T. flour

1½ tsp. raspberry flavoring

1 tsp. grated lemon peel

¼ C. lemon juice

1 C. skim milk

Powdered sugar

Fill a large roasting pan with ½" hot tap water; place in center of oven. Preheat oven to 350°. Place about 5 raspberries in the bottom of eight 6-ounce custard cups; set aside. Into two bowls, separate the yolks and whites of eggs, discarding one yolk. In a medium mixing bowl, beat the four egg whites with an electric mixer at medium speed until foamy. Gradually beat in 2 tablespoons of sugar until stiff shiny peaks form when beaters are lifted; set aside. In a large bowl, use the same beaters to beat three yolks with remaining ½ cup plus 2 tablespoons sugar until mixture is light. Add flour, flavoring, lemon peel and lemon juice; beat until blended. Gradually beat in milk. With a wire whisk, gently fold beaten egg whites into yolk mixture just until combined. Divide batter among prepared custard cups, filling them to the top. Place cups in hot water in a roasting pan. Bake for 24 minutes or until cakes are puffed and golden brown on top. Serve warm or at room temperature, sprinkled with powdered sugar and topped with a few remaining berries.

Serving size: *1 custard cup*
Calories: *142*
Fat: *2.2 g*

Strawberry Cream Pie

Makes 8 servings

2½ C. sliced strawberries

¼ C. sugar

1 env. unflavored gelatin powder

2 T. frozen limeade or lemonade concentrate, thawed

3 egg whites, slightly beaten

3 T. orange juice, divided

1 (3 oz.) pkg. ladyfingers, split

1½ C. light whipped topping

Additional sliced strawberries, optional

Place 2½ cups strawberries into a blender container or food processor. Cover and blend until nearly smooth to get 1½ cups; set aside. In a medium saucepan, combine sugar and gelatin. Stir in blended strawberries and limeade concentrate. Cover and cook over medium heat, stirring constantly, until mixture bubbles and gelatin is dissolved. Stir a spoonful of hot gelatin mixture into beaten egg whites. Slowly add about half of gelatin mixture to egg whites until warmed, then return mixture to saucepan. Cook over low heat for 3 minutes or until slightly thickened, stirring constantly. Do not boil. Pour mixture into a medium bowl and stir in 1 tablespoon orange juice. Chill for 2 hours or until mixture mounds when spooned; stir occasionally. Meanwhile, cut half of the split ladyfingers in half crosswise and stand them on end around the outside edge of a 9" springform pan, rounded sides out. Arrange remaining split ladyfingers in the bottom of pan. Drizzle with remaining 2 tablespoons orange juice. Fold whipped topping into chilled strawberry mixture and spoon into prepared pan. Cover and chill for 2 hours or until set. If desired, garnish with additional sliced strawberries before serving.

Serving size: *1 piece*
Calories: *135*
Fat: *1.9 g*

Easy Double-Orange Dessert

Makes 4 servings

2 large oranges

½ C. nonfat vanilla or plain yogurt

1 T. frozen orange juice concentrate, thawed

3 T. semi-sweet or dark chocolate chips

½ tsp. vegetable oil

Peel oranges and separate the segments. If desired, use a sharp knife to remove all membranes; set aside. In a small bowl, mix together yogurt and orange juice concentrate. Spoon 2 tablespoons of yogurt mixture on each of four dessert plates or bowls. Arrange about 5 orange segments over yogurt mixture. In a small microwave-safe bowl, heat chocolate chips with oil for 20 to 30 seconds; stir and repeat until chocolate is melted and smooth. Drizzle chocolate in thin lines over oranges and serve.

Serving size: *about ¾ cup*
Calories: *110*
Fat: *3 g*

How-to Tip

When cooking with extracts, it's best to add the extract at the end of the cooking time to retain the most flavor. Frozen or refrigerated desserts require more extract than room temperature ones because cold temperatures dull the taste buds.

Two-Layer Pumpkin Cheesecake

Makes 8 servings

⅓ C. graham cracker crumbs

2 (8 oz.) pkgs. fat-free cream cheese, softened

½ C. sugar

½ tsp. vanilla extract

2 eggs

½ C. canned pumpkin puree

¼ tsp. ground cinnamon

Dash of ground nutmeg

½ C. sugar-free, fat-free whipped topping

Preheat oven to 325°. Generously coat a 9" pie pan with nonstick cooking spray. Sprinkle graham cracker crumbs over bottom of pan; set aside. In a large mixing bowl, combine cream cheese, sugar and vanilla; beat with an electric mixer at medium speed until well blended. Add eggs; mix until blended, but do not over-beat. Remove 1 cup of batter and add pumpkin, cinnamon and nutmeg; stir and set mixture aside. Pour remaining plain batter over crust in pan. Top with pumpkin batter. Bake for 40 minutes or until center is almost set. Cool completely, then refrigerate for 3 hours or overnight. Cut into eight slices. Before serving, top each piece with about 1 tablespoon of whipped topping.

Serving size: *1 piece*
Calories: *148*
Fat: *2.2 g*

Espresso Baked Custard

Makes 4 servings

1½ C. 1% milk

2 eggs, beaten

3 T. sugar substitute such as granulated Splenda

2 tsp. espresso powder or instant decaffeinated coffee

1 tsp. vanilla extract

Ground cinnamon

Lemon twists

In a medium bowl, whisk together milk, eggs, sugar substitute, espresso powder and vanilla until well blended. Pour mixture into four 6-ounce custard cups and set into a 10″ skillet. Fill skillet with water to ½″ from the tops of custard cups. Bring water to a boil over high heat. Reduce heat to low, cover skillet and simmer for 10 minutes. Remove cups from skillet and cover with plastic wrap touching the surface of custard to prevent a skin from forming on top. Refrigerate for 3 hours or until chilled. Garnish each with a sprinkling of cinnamon and a lemon twist.

Serving size: *1 custard cup*
Calories: *81*
Fat: *3.5 g*

Raspberry No-Bake Dessert

1 (10.5 oz.) loaf angel food cake
2 (0.3 oz.) pkgs. sugar-free raspberry gelatin powder
1 (16 oz.) pkg. frozen unsweetened raspberries, thawed
2 C. 1% milk, cold
1 (1 oz.) pkg. sugar-free, fat-free instant vanilla pudding mix
1 (8 oz.) carton light whipped topping

Cut or tear cake into 1" cubes. Arrange cubes in a single layer in a 9 x 13" dish; set aside. In a large bowl, combine gelatin and 2 cups boiling water; stir for 2 minutes or until dissolved. Stir in raspberries. Pour mixture over cake in pan and gently press down on cake. Refrigerate for about 1 hour or until set. In a medium bowl, whisk together milk and pudding mix for 2 minutes or until slightly thickened. Spoon mixture over set gelatin layer. Spread whipped topping over pudding layer. Refrigerate until serving time. Cut into pieces.

Serving size: *1 piece*
Calories: *74*
Fat: *2 g*

Chocolate Crepes

Makes about 16 crepes

1 C. skim milk

½ C. fat-free evaporated milk

2 egg whites

1 egg

1 C. flour

¼ C. sugar

¼ C. unsweetened cocoa powder

½ tsp. salt

Prepared Raspberry Sauce (or other filling of choice)

Fat-free whipped topping

Fresh berries, optional

Powdered sugar, optional

In a small mixing bowl, blend milk, evaporated milk, egg whites and egg. In another bowl, stir together flour, sugar, cocoa powder and salt. Add flour mixture to milk mixture, whisking together until smooth. Cover and refrigerate batter for 1 hour. Prepare desired filling and set aside. To cook crepes, coat an 8" nonstick skillet with nonstick cooking spray; place over medium heat. Stir crepe batter and pour a scant 3 tablespoons into skillet; tilt pan to spread batter evenly. Cook until top appears dry; turn over and cook 15 to 20 seconds longer. Remove crepe to a wire rack to cool. Repeat with remaining batter, using cooking spray as needed. Stack cooled crepes with waxed paper in between. To serve, spoon a portion of Raspberry Sauce over each crepe and roll up. Top with whipped topping, a fresh berry and a sprinkle of powdered sugar.

Raspberry Sauce: In a small saucepan, mix 4½ teaspoons cornstarch with ⅓ cup sugar; set aside. In a blender container, puree 3½ cups raspberries with 1 cup water until smooth. Strain pureed mixture into saucepan, discarding seeds. Boil mixture for 2 minutes or until thickened, stirring constantly. Transfer to a small bowl and chill. Spoon into crepes before rolling up.

Serving size: 1 filled crepe
Calories: 105
Fat: 0.5 g

French Crepes

Makes 8 servings

¾ C. skim milk
½ C. flour
¼ C. egg substitute
Dash of salt
Prepared Strawberry-Cream Filling (or other filling of choice)
Fresh sliced strawberries, optional

In a medium bowl, whisk together milk, flour, egg substitute and salt until smooth. Coat a 6" skillet with nonstick cooking spray; place over medium heat. Pour 2 tablespoons of batter into pan, tilting skillet to spread batter evenly. Brown crepe on one side for about 60 seconds or until top appears dry. Loosen edges with a spatula and invert skillet to remove crepe. Spray skillet again and repeat to make eight crepes. To serve, spoon a portion of Strawberry-Cream Filling on each crepe and roll up. Top with fresh strawberries, if desired.

Strawberry-Cream Filling: In a medium saucepan over low heat, combine 4 cups sliced strawberries and 2 teaspoons sugar; cook for 5 minutes or until berries are soft and juice forms. Cool slightly. In a blender container, combine ⅔ cup nonfat cottage cheese, ¼ cup fat-free plain yogurt, ¼ teaspoon ground cinnamon and 2 more teaspoons sugar; blend until smooth. Spoon into crepes before rolling up.

Serving size: 1 filled crepe
Calories: 95
Fat: 0 g

How-to Tip

To freeze unfilled crepes, stack them flat with waxed paper separating layers. Wrap in plastic, pack in an airtight container and freeze.

Stained Glass Pie

1 (0.3 oz.) pkg. sugar-free strawberry gelatin powder

1½ C. Fiber One bran cereal

¼ C. light whipped butter, melted (40% fat)

4 packets Splenda

1 tsp. ground cinnamon

4 (3.2 oz.) sugar-free orange gelatin snack cups

4 (3.2 oz.) sugar-free lemon-lime gelatin snack cups

4 (3.2 oz.) sugar-free raspberry, strawberry or cherry gelatin snack cups

1½ C. free whipped topping

Preheat oven to 350°. Coat the bottom of a 9" springform pan with nonstick cooking spray; set aside. In a large bowl, combine strawberry gelatin powder with 1 cup boiling water; stir for 2 minutes or until completely dissolved. Add ½ cup cold water, stir well and refrigerate for 45 minutes or until slightly thickened. Meanwhile, using a blender or food processor, grind cereal to a crumb consistency and set aside. In a medium bowl, combine melted butter and 2 tablespoons water. Add cereal crumbs, Splenda and cinnamon, stirring until well mixed. Spread crumb mixture in bottom of prepared pan, pressing down firmly to make a crust. Bake crust for 10 minutes. Remove and cool completely. Remove orange gelatin from the plastic snack cups and cut gelatin into ½" cubes; place cubes in a bowl and refrigerate. Repeat with lemon-lime and raspberry gelatin. When strawberry gelatin has thickened slightly, add whipped topping and whisk together until completely blended. Gently stir in all gelatin cubes. Lightly spray the sides of springform pan with nonstick cooking spray. Then spread gelatin mixture evenly over cooled crust. Refrigerate for 3 hours or until firm. To serve, slide a knife around pan edge, remove pan sides and cut pie into eight wedges.

Serving size: *1 wedge*
Calories: *90*
Fat: *2.9 g*

Lime Chiffon Pie

Makes 8 servings

3 egg whites, room temperature

⅛ tsp. cream of tartar

⅓ C. plus 1 T. honey, divided

1½ tsp. vanilla extract, divided

1 env. unflavored gelatin powder

3 T. lime juice

2 egg yolks

½ C. nonfat evaporated milk, chilled

Green food coloring, optional

4 thin lime slices

Whipped topping, optional

Preheat oven to 250°. Coat a 9" pie pan with nonstick cooking spray and a light dusting of flour; set aside. In a large mixing bowl, use an electric mixer to beat egg whites until foamy. Add cream of tartar, 1 tablespoon honey and ½ teaspoon vanilla; beat at high speed until stiff peaks form. Spread mixture on bottom and sides of prepared pie pan. Bake for 30 to 35 minutes or until golden brown. Let meringue pie crust cool. To prepare pie filling, sprinkle gelatin over lime juice in a bowl; set aside for 5 minutes to soften. In the top of a double boiler, beat together egg yolks and remaining ⅓ cup honey. Beat in gelatin mixture and set pan over hot water. Cook over low heat, beating until gelatin dissolves, about 7 minutes. Remove from heat and beat in remaining 1 teaspoon vanilla. Allow mixture to cool. In a large chilled mixing bowl, beat evaporated milk until it reaches the consistency of whipped cream. Fold in lime mixture and food coloring. Spread in pie shell and refrigerate until set. Slice into wedges and garnish with lime slices and whipped topping, if desired.

Serving size: *1 wedge*
Calories: *92*
Fat: *1.3 g*

Pudding-Filled Cream Puffs

Makes 16 servings

½ C. shortening

⅛ tsp. salt

1 C. sifted flour

4 eggs

1 (1 oz.) pkg. sugar-free, fat-free instant pudding mix, any flavor

2 C. skim milk

Powdered sugar

Preheat oven to 450°. In a medium saucepan over medium-high heat, combine shortening, salt and 1 cup boiling water; bring mixture to a boil. Reduce heat and add flour all at once, stirring vigorously until mixture pulls away from the pan and forms a ball. Remove from heat and add eggs, one at a time, beating thoroughly after each addition. Beat until mixture is thick, shiny and breaks from the spoon. Spoon dough on ungreased baking sheets, about 3" apart to make 16 puffs. Bake for 20 minutes, then reduce heat to 350° and bake for 20 minutes more or until golden and hollow-sounding when tapped. Cool completely. Meanwhile, in a medium bowl, combine pudding mix and milk; beat until blended and thick. To fill, cut off tops of puffs and pull out filaments of soft dough. Fill puffs with pudding. Replace tops and sprinkle with powdered sugar.

Serving size: *1 filled puff*
Calories: *113*
Fat: *8.6 g*

Variation

• *Puffs may also be filled with custard, fresh fruit, whipped cream, pie filling, sweetened fat-free cream cheese or lemon curd. Drizzle chocolate or caramel syrup on top. If you use rich fillings, make the puffs smaller.*

Mouth-Watering
Miniatures

Purchase small dessert dishes and drink glasses, with or without stems, to serve these desserts beautifully. Restaurant supply stores carry a wide variety, but don't forget about estate sales, discount stores and your own cupboards. Look for sherbet dishes; sherry, shot, or martini glasses; mini-martini glasses; clear or colored condiment cups; and glass votive holders. Use sizes ranging from 2 to 6 ounces. The richer the dessert, the smaller the serving should be for calorie-conscious enjoyment.

Cranberry Parfaits

Makes 12 servings (using 3.5 oz. dishes)

1 (16 oz.) can whole-berry cranberry sauce
1 C. light cranberry juice drink
½ tsp. grated orange peel
1 (0.3 oz.) pkg. sugar-free raspberry gelatin powder
1 (12 oz.) can low-fat evaporated milk, chilled
1 tsp. vanilla extract
Whole cranberries, optional

Chill a mixing bowl and electric beaters in the freezer. Meanwhile, in a medium saucepan over medium heat, combine cranberry sauce, cranberry juice drink and orange peel; bring mixture to a boil, stirring until cranberry sauce is melted. Remove from heat and stir in gelatin until dissolved. Refrigerate until mixture is the consistency of egg whites, stirring occasionally. In the chilled mixing bowl, combine evaporated milk and vanilla. Beat at high speed until soft peaks form. Add to thickened gelatin mixture and fold in gently until blended. Spoon into miniature dessert cups and chill for 1 to 2 hours or until set. If desired, garnish with fresh whole cranberries before serving.

Serving size: *1 dessert dish*
Calories: *95*
Fat: *0.6 g*

Frozen Chocolate-Raspberry Cups

Makes 12 servings (using 3.5 to 4 oz. glasses)

1 C. 1% cottage cheese

¾ C. skim milk

⅓ C. raspberry spreadable fruit, no sugar added

1 (1.4 oz.) sugar-free instant chocolate pudding mix

1 (8 oz.) carton sugar-free, fat-free whipped topping, thawed

2 (1 oz.) squares semi-sweet chocolate, melted

12 fresh raspberries

In a blender container, combine cottage cheese, milk and spreadable fruit; cover and blend until smooth. Add pudding mix; cover and process until smooth and well blended. Pour mixture into a large bowl. Fold in whipped topping. Spoon mixture into dessert cups. Drizzle with melted chocolate. Cover and freeze for 8 hours or overnight. Let stand at room temperature for 10 to 15 minutes before serving. Garnish each with a raspberry before serving.

Serving size: *1 dessert dish*
Calories: *95*
Fat: *1.7 g*

Pretty Peaches

1 C. plain low-fat yogurt

1 T. honey

½ tsp. lemon juice

3 T. minced crystallized ginger

2 ripe peaches

1 C. sugar-free, fat-free whipped topping

Dash of nutmeg, optional

In a small bowl, mix together yogurt, honey and lemon juice. Fold in ginger. Peel, pit and chop peaches into small pieces. Fold peaches into yogurt mixture. Spoon into serving dishes, cover and chill at least 1 hour. Garnish each with a dollop of whipped topping seasoned with nutmeg before serving, if desired.

Serving size: *1 dessert dish*
Calories: *62*
Fat: *0.5 g*

Apricot Nectar Fluff

Makes about 8 servings (using 3 to 3.5 oz. dishes)

1 egg yolk
¼ C. quick-cooking tapioca
¾ C. apricot nectar
¾ C. unsweetened pineapple juice
1 T. lemon juice
Sugar substitute equal to ½ C. sugar
½ tsp. vanilla extract
¼ tsp. orange extract
Egg white powder equal to 2 whites
3 maraschino cherries, sliced thin, optional

In a medium saucepan, lightly beat the egg yolk. Add tapioca, apricot nectar, pineapple juice, lemon juice and ¾ cup water to saucepan; mix well. Let mixture stand for 5 minutes. Bring mixture to a boil over medium heat, cooking and stirring constantly for 6 to 8 minutes. Remove from heat. Add sugar substitute, vanilla and orange extracts; mix well. In a small mixing bowl, combine egg white powder with water according to package instructions. Using an electric mixer at high speed, beat until soft peaks form. Gradually add tapioca mixture, stirring quickly only until blended. Spoon into dessert cups and serve immediately, or chill before serving. Garnish with sliced maraschino cherries, if desired.

Serving size: *1 dessert dish*
Calories: *54*
Fat: *1.3 g*

Chocolate-Raspberry Mousse Deluxe

Makes 8 servings (using 2 oz. sherry glasses)

½ C. butter, softened

⅓ C. sugar

2 (1 oz.) squares semi-sweet baking chocolate,
  melted and cooled

½ C. egg substitute

2 tsp. raspberry liqueur, optional

1 C. raspberries

Grated chocolate bar, optional

In a small mixing bowl, use an electric mixer at medium speed to beat together butter and sugar until creamy, scraping bowl often. Add melted chocolate and beat until well mixed. Add egg substitute and continue beating until very creamy. Stir in raspberry liqueur. Place 2 raspberries in the bottom of each serving dish. Top each with about 1½ tablespoons chocolate mousse, several more raspberries and another layer of chocolate mousse. Garnish each with a sprinkling of grated chocolate and another raspberry.

Serving size: *1 dessert dish*
Calories: *123*
Fat: *9.2 g*

Mini Strawberry Shortcake

Makes 2 servings (using 4 to 5 oz. dessert glasses)

1 T. sugar-free strawberry preserves

1 shortcake dessert cup, torn into small pieces

⅓ C. sliced strawberries

⅓ C. nonfat vanilla ice cream

¼ C. fat-free aerosol whipped topping

In a small bowl, mix preserves with 1½ teaspoons hot water to make a strawberry sauce; set aside. Place half of the shortcake pieces in each dessert glass. Top with a scant tablespoonful of strawberries. Place half of the ice cream into each glass, on top of strawberries. Place another spoonful of strawberries on ice cream, pressing down lightly. Drizzle half of the strawberry sauce over each serving and top with about 2 tablespoons whipped topping. Arrange remaining strawberries over whipped topping. Serve immediately.

Serving size: *1 dessert glass*
Calories: *95*
Fat: *1 g*

Mini Hot
Fudge Sundaes

1 (2") brownie

½ C. fat-free vanilla ice cream

4 tsp. hot fudge topping, warmed

2 T. fat-free aerosol whipped topping

2 maraschino cherries with stems

Cut the brownie into small pieces. Place 2 to 3 pieces of brownie into each dessert dish. Top each with a ¼-cup scoop of ice cream. Arrange remaining brownie pieces around ice cream in each dish and drizzle with 2 teaspoons of warm fudge topping. Top each serving with 1 tablespoon whipped topping and a maraschino cherry.

Serving size: *1 dessert dish*
Calories: *147*
Fat: *4.5 g*

White Chocolate Peppermint Cups

Makes 4 to 5 servings (using 4 to 5 oz. dessert dishes)

4 oz. fat-free cream cheese, softened

½ C. plus 2 T. skim milk

½ (1 oz.) pkg. sugar-free, fat-free instant white chocolate pudding mix

1 C. light whipped topping, divided

1 (½ oz.) candy cane or 3 hard peppermint candies, crushed, divided

In a medium mixing bowl, whisk cream cheese until creamy. Beat in 2 tablespoons milk, until well blended. Add pudding mix and remaining ½ cup milk; beat until smooth and creamy, about 1 minute. Fold in ¾ cup whipped topping and half of the crushed candy. Spoon mixture into dessert dishes and sprinkle remaining crushed candy on top.

Serving size: *1 dessert dish*
Calories: *97*
Fat: *1.6 g*

Variation

• *Substitute sugar-free, fat-free instant chocolate pudding mix in place of white chocolate pudding mix.*

Warm Rhubarb Compote with Yogurt Timbales

Makes 7 servings (using 5 to 6 oz. dishes)

2 C. low-fat vanilla yogurt
1 lb. fresh rhubarb stems, leaves removed
½ C. currant jelly

Spoon equal amounts of yogurt into seven 3-ounce paper cups. Place cups in the freezer for about 1 hour or until semi-frozen. (If making this dessert in advance, freeze completely and then remove cups from freezer about 15 minutes before serving.) Preheat oven to 400°. Wash rhubarb and cut stems into 1½" lengths on the bias. In a shallow 8" baking dish, combine rhubarb and jelly, stirring until pieces are coated. Bake for about 35 minutes or until rhubarb is tender, stirring twice. Remove from oven and cool for 5 minutes. Spoon warm rhubarb into seven dessert dishes. Unmold frozen yogurt timbales and set one on top of the rhubarb in each dish.

Serving size: 1 dessert dish
Calories: 111
Fat: 0.6 g

Apricot-Cheesecake Tartlets

3 (1 oz.) squares bittersweet chocolate

½ tsp. shortening

1 (1.9 oz.) pkg. frozen miniature phyllo tart shells

1 (3 oz.) pkg. light cream cheese, softened

2 T. sour cream

2 T. powdered sugar

2 tsp. apricot nectar

3 T. dried apricots, cut into thin strips

1 to 1½ tsp. grated chocolate

In a small microwave-safe bowl, melt bittersweet chocolate and shortening; stir until smooth. Brush melted chocolate over the inside of tart shells, covering the bottom and sides with a thin layer. Refrigerate for 15 minutes or until chocolate is set. Meanwhile, in a small mixing bowl, use an electric mixer at low speed to beat together cream cheese, sour cream and powdered sugar until smooth. Beat in nectar. Spoon mixture into shells, cover and chill for at least 20 minutes. Just before serving, top tarts with apricot strips and a sprinkling of grated chocolate.

Serving size: *1 tartlet*
Calories: *72*
Fat: *3.9 g*

How-to Tip

Serve tartlets with a small chilled dessert cup of apricot or vanilla yogurt, which will add calories, or a cup of flavored coffee.

Miniature Cannoli

⅔ C. part-skim ricotta cheese

2 T. powdered sugar

2 tsp. Grand Marnier liqueur

2 tsp. grated orange peel

1 T. miniature semi-sweet chocolate chips

1 (1.9 oz.) pkg. frozen miniature phyllo tart shells

In a small mixing bowl, beat ricotta cheese with an electric mixer at medium speed for 2 minutes. Add powdered sugar and liqueur; beat for 2 to 3 minutes or until mixture is smooth. Mix in orange peel and chocolate chips. Chill mixture for 1 hour. Spoon by rounded teaspoonfuls into each tart shell and serve immediately.

Serving size: *3 tarts*
Calories: *126*
Fat: *6.9 g*

Party Parfait Buffets

Throw a party and let your guests make their own miniature dessert parfait. Arrange a buffet line by displaying a variety of small dessert dishes (2½ to 5 ounces) and prepared parfait ingredients in the order listed here. Then invite guests to choose their favorites and assemble their own perfectly-pleasing party parfait! Calories in each parfait will vary, but by using small dishes and low-calorie ingredients for the main parfait layers, everyone will come away a winner. Make homemade creamy and crunchy layers with the recipes which follow, or use conveniently packaged dessert cups for quick-fixes. The charts will provide an endless supply of ideas.

Crunchy Layers

Use one portion for a base layer and a smaller portion as a sprinkling on top, if desired.

Crunchy Layers	Serving Size	Calories
Crunchy Nut-Oatmeal Streusel (recipe on page 117)	1 T.	48
Peanut Butter Graham Cracker Crumbs (recipe on page 118)	1 T	28
Coconut Graham Cracker Crumbs (recipe on page 118)	1 T.	33
Plain Graham Cracker Crumbs (recipe on page 118)	1 T.	16
Crushed vanilla wafers	1 wafer	17
Crushed chocolate graham crackers	1 square	16
Crushed cookie (use ½ cookie for base, ½ cookie for topping)		
Oreo (regular)	1 cookie	53
Iced oatmeal (2½")	1 cookie	65
Chocolate chip (1 oz., regular)	1 cookie	100
Peanut butter (1 oz., low-fat)	1 cookie	105
Toasted coconut or nuts	1 T.	36
Crunchy cereals, such as Grape Nuts	1 T.	25
Crumbled rice cakes (any flavor)	¼ cake	13

Creamy Layers

Use 2 to 4 tablespoons of creamy layer per parfait.

Note: 1 (4-serving) package of instant pudding made with skim milk yields 2 cups pudding.

Smooth and Creamy Layers	Serving Size	Calories
Pudding, sugar-free, fat-free 　　Chocolate, Vanilla 　　Banana Cream, Butterscotch 　　White Chocolate, Cheesecake	 2 to 4 T. 2 to 4 T. 2 to 4 T.	 20 to 40 24 to 48 24 to 48
Pudding, regular 　　Chocolate, Vanilla 　　Pistachio, Cheesecake 　　Banana Cream, Butterscotch, 　　　White Chocolate	 2 to 4 T. 2 to 4 T. 2 to 4 T.	 57 to 113 62 to 123 57 to 113
Chocolate Almond Mousse (recipe on page115)	2 to 4 T.	18 to 36
Strawberry Mousse (recipe on page 116)	2 to 4 T.	28 to 55
Creamy Pudding and Pie Filling (recipe on page 11)	¼ C.	74
Whipped toppings (as a separate layer or mixed into pudding) 　　Lite or Free Cool Whip 　　Chocolate Cool Whip 　　Strawberry Cool Whip 　　French Vanilla Cool Whip	 2 to 4 T. 2 to 4 T. 2 to 4 T. 2 to 4 T.	 15 to 40 25 to 50 25 to 50 25 to 50

Fruity Layers

Place a fruit layer on top of the creamy layer using amounts listed.

Fruity Layers	Serving Size	Calories
Canned pie fillings such as cherry, blueberry or apple	2 T.	32 to 70
Fresh fruits, cut into small pieces 　　Strawberries 　　Blueberries 　　Bananas	 ¼ C. slices ¼ C. slices 4 to 5 slices	 11 20 22
Canned fruit 　　Mandarin oranges 　　Peaches 　　Tropical fruit (in light syrup)	 3 to 4 segments 2 to 3 slices 2 to 4 T.	 23 28 20 to 40

Whipped Toppings
Use about 2 tablespoons of topping over previous layer.

Whipped Toppings	Serving Size	Calories
Lite Cool Whip	2 T.	20
Free Cool Whip or regular Dream Whip	2 T.	15
Flavored Cool Whip (Chocolate, Strawberry, French Vanilla)	2 T.	25
Reddi-Wip aerosol topping, fat-free	2 T.	5
Any topping substitutions (recipes on pages 8-9)	2 T.	11 to 35

Syrups & Sauces
Drizzle approximately 1 teaspoon of syrup or sauce over topping.

Syrups and Sauces	Serving Size	Calories
Syrups Chocolate, Strawberry Hot Fudge, Butterscotch, Caramel	1 tsp. 1 tsp.	17 23
Crème de Menthe	1 tsp.	21

Sprinkles
Sprinkle or dust top of parfait with about 1 teaspoon.

Sprinkles or Dustings	Serving Size	Calories
Grated chocolate (candy bars, chocolate chips)	1 tsp.	18
Chopped candy bars (1 miniature = range of 30 to 55 cal each) Reeses peanut butter cup Mint patty Snickers Twix Kit Kat	1 miniature 1 patty 1 miniature 1 miniature 1 miniature	42 30 to 47 43 50 46
Miniature chocolate chips or M&M's	1 tsp.	18
Cookie sprinkles	1 tsp.	20
Colored sugar	½ to 1 tsp	15
Powdered sugar	1 tsp.	8
Unsweetened cocoa powder	½ to 1 tsp.	5
Toasted coconut	1 tsp.	12
Peanuts finely chopped	1 tsp.	18
Any crunchy layers from page 111	1 tsp.	varies

Garnishes
Add a finishing touch with one of these toppers.

Garnishes	Serving Size	Calories
Maraschino cherries	1 cherry	10
M&M's candy	1 single or several miniatures	5 to 10
Cookie wedge (cookie cut in half or quarter, stuck into whipped topping) Oreo Chocolate chip Thin mint	½ cookie ¼ cookie ½ cookie	27 25 18
Peanuts	3 peanuts	20

My Favorite Combos
Record your favorite combos and calories for quick reference.

	Crunchy Layer	Creamy Layer	Fruity Layer	Whipped Topping	Syrup or Sauce	Sprinkles	Garnish	Total Cal.
1								
2								
3								
4								
5								

Easy Chocolate Almond Mousse

Makes about 12 servings (using 3 oz. dishes)

1 (1.4 oz.) pkg. sugar-free, fat-free instant chocolate
  pudding mix
2 C. skim milk
⅛ tsp. almond extract
2 C. free whipped topping, divided
Unsweetened cocoa powder, optional

In a medium bowl, combine pudding mix, milk and extract; whisk for 2 minutes or until well-blended and slightly thickened. Gently fold 1⅔ cups whipped topping into pudding until evenly mixed. Spoon mixture into individual serving dishes and chill for 2 hours or until firm. To serve, place a dollop of whipped topping on each serving and a sprinkling of cocoa powder, if desired. Use as a creamy layer in any party parfait.

Serving size: *1 dessert dish*
Calories: *46*
Fat: *0.1 g*

Strawberry Mousse

Makes about 12 servings (using 3 to 3.5 oz. dishes)

4 C. quartered fresh or frozen unsweetened strawberries
½ C. sugar
1 (1 oz.) pkg. sugar-free, fat-free instant vanilla
   pudding mix
1 (8 oz.) carton reduced-fat whipped topping, thawed
Additional strawberries, optional

In a food processor or blender container, combine strawberries and sugar; cover and process until smooth. Strain and discard seeds. Return strawberry mixture to the food processor and add pudding mix; cover and process until smooth and well blended. Transfer mixture to a large bowl and fold in whipped topping. Spoon mixture into small dessert dishes and chill before serving. If desired, garnish with a small whole or sliced strawberry. Use as a creamy layer in any party parfait.

> **Serving size:** *1 dessert dish*
> **Calories:** *93*
> **Fat:** *2 g*

Crunchy Nut-Oatmeal Streusel

Makes about 1 cup

¼ C. old fashioned oats
¼ C. flour
2 T. brown sugar
2 T. butter, cut into pieces
2 T. chopped pecans or walnuts
½ tsp. ground cinnamon, optional

Preheat oven 300°. In a medium bowl, combine oats, flour and brown sugar. Use a pastry blender or two knives to cut in butter until mixture is crumbly. Stir in chopped pecans and cinnamon, if desired. Spread mixture in a 9 x 13" baking pan and bake for 15 to 20 minutes, stirring every 5 minutes, until mixture is lightly browned. Let mixture cool completely. Use as a crunchy layer or topping in any party parfait.

Serving size: *1 tablespoon*
Calories: *48 calories*
Fat: *2.5g*

Peanut Butter-Graham Cracker Crumbs

Makes about 1 cup

4 (2½") graham cracker squares, crushed

1 T. brown sugar

2 T. smooth peanut butter

3 T. chopped walnuts or pecans

In a medium bowl, combine crushed crackers and brown sugar. Use a pastry blender or two knives to cut in peanut butter until mixture is crumbly. Stir in chopped walnuts. Use as a crunchy layer or topping in any party parfait.

Serving size: *1 tablespoon*
Calories: *28*
Fat: *2 g*

Variations

- **Coconut-Graham Cracker Crumbs**: *Add 3 tablespoons sweetened flaked coconut. (This adds 5 calories and 1.5 gram fat per 1-tablespoon serving.)*
- **Plain Graham Cracker Crumbs**: *Omit peanut butter and mix ingredients as directed. (This takes away 12 calories and 1 gram of fat per 1-tablespoon serving.)*

Quick-Fix Mini Parfaits

Make quick desserts from conveniently-packaged pudding, yogurt or gelatin snack cups and other ingredients. Place the layers of ingredients in sundae dishes that hold 5 to 6 ounces.

Dessert	Layer 1	Layer 2	Layer 3	Layer 4
Banana Split Parfait (145 Calories)	½ sugar-free vanilla pudding cup	½ small banana, sliced	3 T. fat-free whipped topping	2 tsp. semi-sweet chocolate chips, chopped
Banana Crunch Parfait (146 Calories)	½ sugar-free vanilla pudding cup	½ small banana, sliced	1 T. crunchy nut-oatmeal streusel (page 117)	2 T. fat-free whipped topping
Mini Double Chocolate Parfait (148 Calories)	1½ T. peanut butter crumbs mix (page 118)	½ sugar-free chocolate pudding cup	3 T. fat-free whipped topping	2 tsp. M&M's mini baking bits
Chocolate Mint Parfait (146 Calories)	1 sugar-free chocolate mint fudge pudding cup	2 Andes Creme de Menthe Thins, crushed	3 T. fat-free whipped topping	1 maraschino cherry
Cookies-n-Cream Parfait (135 Calories)	1 Chips Ahoy reduced fat chocolate chip cookie	1 Andes Creme de Menthe Thin, crushed	2 T. fat-free whipped topping	1 maraschino cherry
Berry Crunch Parfait (137 Calories)	½ fat-free strawberry yogurt cup	¼ C. strawberries	¼ C. blueberries	1 T. crunchy nut-oatmeal streusel (page 117)
Chocolate-Covered Strawberry Parfait (146 Calories)	½ fat-free strawberry yogurt cup	¼ C. strawberries	3 T. fat-free whipped topping	1 T. chocolate syrup

Mix & Match
Mini Parfaits

Choose your favorite ingredient from each column to create a different layered dessert every time.

Use ½ Pudding Snack Cup (about 3 - 4 T.)	Use 2 T.	Use 2 tsp.	Use 1 tsp.
Sugar-free Banana Fudge Supreme Pudding (30 Calories)	fat-free whipped topping (15 Calories)	peanut butter crumbs mix (19 Calories) (page 118)	coconut, toasted* (12 Calories)
Sugar-free Chocolate Pudding (30 Calories)	peanut butter crumbs mix (56 Calories) (page 118)	coconut, toasted* (24 Calories)	M&M's mini baking chips (24 Calories)
Sugar-free Vanilla Pudding (30 Calories)	sliced banana (17 Calories)	crunchy nut-oatmeal streusel (37 Calories) (page 117)	chopped pecans, toasted* (18 Calories)
Sugar-free Chocolate Mint Fudge Pudding (30 Calories)	Oreo reduced fat cookie, crushed (50 Calories)	fat-free whipped topping (5 Calories)	Andes mint baking chips, chopped (24 Calories)
Sugar-free Dark Chocolate Pudding (30 Calories)	Chips Ahoy reduced fat chocolate chip cookie, crushed (50 Calories)	chocolate whipped topping (9 Calories)	Crème de Menthe (72 proof) (21 Calories)

Use ½ Jello Snack Cup (about 3 - 4 T.)	Use 2 T.	Use 1 T.	Use 1 tsp.
Sugar-free Strawberry Jello (5 Calories)	sliced strawberries (6 Calories)	strawberry whipped topping (13 Calories)	strawberry syrup (17 Calories)
Sugar-free Raspberry Jello (5 Calories)	fat-free vanilla yogurt (25 Calories)	crushed raspberries (8 Calories)	3 whole raspberries (3 Calories)
Sugar-free Kiwi & Berry Jello (5 Calories)	blueberries (10 Calories)	fat-free vanilla yogurt (8 Calories)	1 kiwi fruit slice (10 Calories)
Sugar-free Orange Jello (5 Calories)	fat-free strawberry yogurt (25 Calories)	Grape Nuts cereal (25 Calories)	orange whipped yogurt (18 Calories)
Sugar-free Lemon Lime Jello (5 Calories)	French vanilla Cool Whip (25 Calories)	fat-free lemon yogurt (8 Calories)	maraschino cherry (10 Calories)

INDEX

The Low-Down on Low-Cal

	Page Number	Calories/Serving	Fat/Serving
Creamy Pudding & Pie Filling	11	24	1.7 g
Dieter's Sour Cream	10	9	trace
Low-Cal Whipped Topping	9	12	0 g
Mock Whipped Topping	8	11	trace
Sweetened Condensed Milk Substitute	10	14	0 g
Yogurt-Ricotta Whipped Topping	9	35	1.3 g

Simply Fruity

Balsamic Strawberries over Ice Cream	23	149	2.1 g
Black Cherry Baked Apples	35	146	4.6 g
Blueberry-Stuffed Apples	20	111	0 g
Cran-Peach Blueberry Mold	27	70	0 g
Cran-Raspberry Gelatin	26	148	2 g
Creamy Strawberry-Orange Cups	25	90	0.3 g
Fruit Kabobs with Creamy Dip	18	91	1 g
Grilled Peachy-Pineapple Crisp	34	149	3 g
Honeyed Fruit Kabobs	19	80	0 g
Mango & Cream Parfaits	30	128	1.7 g
Melon-Sorbet Parfaits	29	91	0 g
Peach Tart	33	125	4 g
Pineapple Ambrosia	28	141	5.4 g
Poached Pears with Raspberry Sauce	36	144	0 g
Refreshing Papaya Fluff	32	64	0 g
Refreshing Summer Fruit Blend	24	25	0 g
Spiced Fruit Dip	21	106	11 g
Velvety Chocolate Dip	22	63	0 g
Warm-Weather Fruit Cups	31	96	0 g

INDEX

Frozen Favorites

Cookies & Candy

INDEX

Bars & Cakes

Guest-Worthy Desserts

INDEX